"These days life seems stuck on fast forward, ɪ neck speed. In their book *Staying Focused in the Age of Distraction*, the Hoffman's provide a thought provoking and user-friendly guide for all of us who need to recapture the focus of our lives in a world filled with distractions. The authors put readers in touch with the wisdom of the rich and varied spiritual traditions of Jewish, Christian, and Eastern scholars and mystics. Then they add a healthy dose of the best current clinical views on mindfulness and behavior change to create a helpful series of experiences and exercises that are easy to use. The strategies combined with the interesting and illustrative stories of people that readers will certainly recognize convinced me that by dedicating a few minutes a day we really can overcome the sense of being frazzled and overwhelmed by our daily lives and regain focus, health, and happiness."

—*Carlo C. DiClemente, Ph.D., professor and chair of the Department of Psychology at the University of Maryland, Baltimore County*

With so much of the world trying to capture our attention, it is a major challenge to attend to what matters and tune out what doesn't. *Staying Focused in the Age of Distraction* provides an inspirational and practical approach to changing, including a guide through the stages of change, so that we can become centered on that which matters most in our lives."

—*James O. Prochaska, Ph.D., professor of clinical health and psychology and director of the Cancer Prevention Research Center at the University of Rhode Island in Kingston, RI*

"*Staying Focused in the Age of Distraction* goes beyond homilies and slogans, it uses up-to-date research to give readers practical steps on how they can achieve meaningful change and improvement in their lives."

—*Samuel Knapp, Ph.D., psychologist and author*

"Every once in a great while, a book is written that seems to be synchronized with our lifetime. *Staying Focused in the Age of Distraction* is such a book. This book will lead you on a path of awareness, discovery and hopefully, a meaningful life change. Some self-help books are neither helpful nor teach you much about your true self. This one does both."

—*Salvatore Cullari, Ph.D., author of* Treatment Resistance: A Guide for Practitioners, Foundations of Clinical Psychology and Consulting *and* Psychotherapy: A Practical Guide for Students, Interns and New Professionals

"Your attention is a precious commodity and the competition for it is intense. *Staying Focused in the Age of Distraction* offers help to take charge and manage your attention. Its practical and inspiring approach to getting and staying clear and focused offers hope for more personal fulfillment. Let this be your workbook for positive change."

—*The Rev. Duane H. Fickeisen, parish minister of the Unitarian Universalists of the Cumberland Valley located in Boiling Springs, PA*

"*Staying Focused in the Age of Distraction* is simultaneously inspirational and comforting. The authors gently guide the reader in a "go-at-your-own-pace" fashion to answers that resolve that nagging question so many of us experience in this hustle and hurry life: 'If everything is so great, why do I always feel like I'm missing something?' Make time to read this book, and you'll find answers of your own!"

—*Sharon Hartman, LSW, MBA, director of professional training and education for the Caron Foundation*

staying

focused in

the age of

distraction

How Mindfulness, Prayer & Meditation Can Help You Pay Attention to What Really Matters

ELIZABETH HANSON HOFFMAN, PH.D.
CHRISTOPHER D. HOFFMAN, MSW, LCSW

New Harbinger Publications, Inc.

Distributed in Canada by Raincoast Books

Copyright © 2006 by Elizabeth Hoffman and Christopher Hoffman
New Harbinger Publications, Inc.
5674 Shattuck Avenue
Oakland, CA 94609
www.newharbinger.com

Cover design by Amy Shoup; Acquired by Jess O'Brien;
Cover image by Stockdisc Classic/Getty Images; Edited by Carole Honeychurch;
Text design by Tracy Marie Carlson

Library of Congress Cataloging-in-Publication Data

Hoffman, Elizabeth Hanson.
  Staying focused in the age of distraction : how mindfulness, prayer, and meditation can help you pay attention to what really matters / Elizabeth Hanson Hoffman and Christopher Hoffman.
       p. cm.
  Includes bibliographical references.
  ISBN-13: 978-1-57224-433-7
  ISBN-10: 1-57224-433-X
  1. Attention. 2. Attention—Religious aspects. 3. Meditation. I. Hoffman, Christopher Douglas. II. Title.
  BF321.H64 2006
  153.1'532—dc22
                                                    2006002611

08   07   06

10   9   8   7   6   5   4   3   2   1

First printing

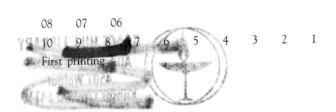

Dedicated to Elizabeth, Edwin, Pearl, John, and Mei Mei.
You are our inspiration to stay focused.

Contents

Preface

Every once in a while a book comes along that hits the sweet spot. If you've found your way to *Staying Focused*, then you've found one of those books.

All too often in today's task-oriented, goal-focused world, we feel the tug of that nagging question on the edge of our consciousness: "I have so much, why aren't I happy?" That feeling of something missing—the joy, zest, and enthusiasm that we started out with have gotten lost along the way.

If you've read your share of "how to" books—enthusiastic about the concepts but confused about the application—here is the book for you. The Hoffmans have taken research and professional and personal experience and managed to shine a light on the key elements we need to know and practice for lasting happiness, meaning, and peace of mind. Illustrated with dozens of anecdotes that portray a variety of paths, each of us is encouraged, chapter by chapter, to take the risk to find our own path.

Simultaneously inspirational and comforting, the authors of *Staying Focused* provide a "go-at-your-own-pace" approach to finding your way to quality living and what really matters in your life. The book is rich in practical guidance so that the reader can follow a step-by-step map to discover the missing links. We each find our way. Every journey is different—uniquely our own. I invite you to embark on yours.

—Sharon Hartman, LSW, MBA
Director of Professional Training & Education
Caron Foundation

Acknowledgments

WITH GRATITUDE

First, I am grateful to my coauthor and son, Chris. We spent hundreds of hours working separately and together to bring this project to completion. If nothing further were to happen as a result of this effort, the process has been fulfilling and reinforcing in and of itself. Chris' loving wife, Pearl, encouraged and supported this project from the beginning. Without her, it would have not been possible. Their children, John and Mei Mei, have been a source of love and joy.

Elizabeth, my daughter, was a shining ray of light. She read drafts, completed exercises, and provided valuable feedback. She also gets credit for inspiring the title. My sister, Isabel, and my Uncle Bob were loving and supportive.

Many people helped to create this book. Leslie Carr spent hours editing and, with kindness, provided guidance. Sharon Hartman, Sal Cullari, Carlo DiClemente, Sam Knapp, James Prochaska, and Rick Small are colleagues who generously gave us input and encouragement. I am appreciative to Marcia Goldberg and Richard Michaels for inspiring me years ago, when the book was only a vague idea. Steve Costa and Rabbi Brian Michelson also helped us, and we thank them.

Duane Fickeisen and Judy Welles, pastors of the Unitarian Universalists of the Cumberland Valley, offered consistent support. Many members of this fellowship provided their experience and insight. I thank Dot Everhart, Alan and Kit Franklin, Carol Lindsay, Doug and Janet Spencer, Diane Reed, Paula Terry, and others who gave freely of themselves.

I am grateful to the therapists, staff, and my clients at Hoffman Psychological Associates. I have learned so much from them in the past twenty-one years.

The editors at New Harbinger believed in this project and gently guided us every step of the way. It was a pleasure to work with them.

Finally, I am grateful to Edwin Glasgow, whose encouragement, love, and support inspire me on a daily basis. I thank him for his patience and I promise to go sailing soon!

—Elizabeth Hoffman

Introduction

That which dominates our imaginations and our
thoughts will determine our lives, and character.
Therefore, it behooves us to be careful about what we
worship, for what we are worshipping we are becoming.

—Ralph Waldo Emerson*

Writing these first words is an act of faith: faith that this book will help you to stay focused on what matters in your life. You can become more aware about what lights your fire and keeps it burning. What will you be doing next month or next year? How will your life be different? How will it be the same? For clues, look around you today. With whom are

* Reprinted by permission of Random Houes, Inc.

you spending your time? Where do you devote your energies? Choose carefully. Your focus becomes your life.

Skills are available for your journey. You can develop your intuition to become conscious of what adds purpose and meaning to your life. You can learn to overcome distractions that keep you stuck. You can incorporate your sense of purpose into your daily activities. You can live with the joy, passion, and contentment that comes from "living right," whatever that means to you. It's true—you can increase and sustain your happiness and well-being. But first you have to learn how to manage your attention.

YOUR ATTENTION

We know that corporate entities pay millions of dollars each year to capture and manage your attention in sophisticated advertising campaigns. If others are spending a fortune to compete for your attention, don't you think you should have some tools to control your awareness?

If you were more conscious about where you put your attention, how would your life be different? Would you be spending more time with your family or pursuing additional education? Which of your natural talents, strengths, and interests would you choose to develop? How would you prioritize what is dear to you? Attention is a precious resource, and it has great value. What is truly worthy of your focus?

On average, unhappy people spend twice as much time focused on the negative aspects of their lives and surroundings as they do on the positive aspects (Lyubomirsky 1994). People who ruminate like this are 70 percent less likely to feel satisfied with their lives (Scott and McIntosh 1999). Happy people focus on information that brightens their futures. It has been shown that when we define our purpose in life and what is meaningful to us, we are more likely to feel satisfied. When we allow external forces to do this, we tend to feel lost and out of control. Depression and anxiety often follow.

What is your purpose in life? What really matters to you? These questions are eternal and universal. Finding the time and developing the awareness to answer these questions can be a daunting task. When your life purpose is more clearly defined, you are likely to feel greater satisfaction with your life. This is true for both young people (Lepper 1996) and for older people (Rahman and Khaleque 1996). In addition, regardless of religious affiliation, people with strongly held spiritual beliefs are more satisfied than those without spiritual beliefs (Gerwood, LeBanc, and Piazza 1998). Taking your life purpose seriously while taking yourself lightly is a challenge. Maintaining the motivation to stay on your path is also a challenge.

Positive Psychology

The inspiration for this book comes from the clinical experience of the authors combined with volumes of academic research, particularly in the area of *positive psychology*. This is a recent term for an area of psychology that is based on humanism, spiritual studies, and *constructivism* (Mahoney 2002). Constructivism emphasizes that we co-create our reality by how we engage with the world. Our experience forms our narrative—the story we tell ourselves about the world and our place in it (Salzberg 2002). Hope and meaning are areas explored by constructivism and positive psychology (Mahoney 2002).

Positive psychology looks at what is right with people instead of what is wrong with them (Snyder and Lopez 2002). The research addressing the strengths and virtues of ordinary people has advanced rapidly in the past five years, and we are learning more about what makes life worth living (Gable and Haidt 2005). We have included some of these exciting strategies for how to live a happier, more resilient and meaningful life.

Staying Focused in the Age of Distraction explores the research areas of spirituality and mindfulness. You will learn how to tune out nonessentials and focus on meaningful activities, relationships, and intrinsically satisfying goals. Then we guide you through the specifics of how to create a program for self-change so you can begin to take the necessary steps to live a life of focus, gaining a sense of deep meaning and satisfaction despite all of the forces set upon diverting your energy.

This approach may sound overwhelming. It's true that it will require energy and dedication from you. But it is important to remember that you don't need to do it all at once. The jacket of this book may need to collect some dust at times along the way. That's okay. We take a broad sweep across many ideas. Begin by just thinking about these ideas, then, as you feel ready, go deeper into their application for your life by writing in your journal and doing additional reading in areas that intrigue you.

This book is meant to be a guide for deep and meaningful life change. In our experience, this type of change seldom comes quickly or without effort. We think the journey is a fascinating one. This is your day. This is your energy. The breath you take is your own. The thoughts you have are yours. They are precious because this is the raw material of a life—of *your* life. Where do you want your energy going? What do you want to think about? How do you want to live? It is this stuff that matters most because without asking these basic questions about your life, you can end up living a life that is guided by marketers, news media, and other people's agendas. One of the deepest tragedies is to live a life that is not your own.

YOUR PROCESS

Most of us have felt a pull from the future, a desire to be more than we are today. How do we create a space for change and build the motivation to sustain us in our journey? The first section of this book describes self-monitoring and ways to organize yourself for your new practices and for focusing your attention. We encourage you to measure your progress by periodically reviewing the exercises you have completed in this section. This will provide valuable insight. The review also will give you reinforcement as you start to see changes in the way you relate your new practices and attention management to everyday living.

We create our way of seeing the world. Thich Nhat Hanh (2003), a noted Buddhist monk, believes that our minds are like gardens and that the seeds we nurture will be the seeds that grow. We can cultivate anger and violence or we can nourish understanding, love, and compassion, even in the face of conflict. What we focus on becomes our life, and managing our attention is crucial.

We will explore the topic of mindfulness, since it is closely associated with the concept of attention. With the extreme competition for your attention from advertisers, increasing workloads, and personal demands, you can become mindless by default, not by design. Mindlessness results in living on automatic pilot. You lose your individuality and your ability to recognize and contribute your unique gifts in a meaningful way.

You'll learn attention-management techniques in chapter 2, which can help you reduce clutter in your mind by teaching you how to shift your focus from unwanted thoughts. This allows you to have more control over where you expend your energy. You will also come to understand how strategies such as mindful breathing and focusing skills can incorporate all the senses. These approaches will help you learn to center yourself so that you may derive maximum benefit, not just from this book, but from your new, more focused life. Throughout the book we recommend exercises to clarify your thought patterns and strengthen your attention-management skills. We discuss the value of writing in your journal. In addition, you will learn ways to remind yourself to stay mindful in your daily routine.

Next, in chapter 3, you will identify activities that are interesting and meaningful to you. Connections will be made from your childhood to the present time. You will identify your activities in the areas of work and achievement as well as relationships and intimacy. From these activities you will develop a blueprint for increased meaning in your life. Your blueprint creates a firm foundation and structure for building a life that works for you. It's easy to say "But I don't have the time for all of this!" We suggest ways to simplify and free up time and mental energy for more mindful practices.

Then, in chapter 4, you will connect your blueprint of meaningful activity with your spiritual practices, beliefs, and experiences. We will look at the research about the different forms of prayer and examine who prays, for what reasons, and to what end. Writing a spiritual auto-biography helps you to clarify these connections and strengthens your motivation to sharpen your focus as you include more spiritual prac-tices and meaningful activity into your daily life. The exercises you complete in this chapter are your personal assessments. We do not promote any particular religious affiliation.

You will learn what research has to say about the rewards that come from increasing mindfulness, spiritual practices, and living a happier life filled with meaning. Improvements in physical and mental health are some of the benefits to be enjoyed. There is also a section on how religion can hurt; we add cautionary notes that you might find interesting.

There are many facets to your sense of well-being. Chapter 5 will help you to assess your physical, emotional, and spiritual life and the factors that enhance your well-being in those areas. We include a section on a helpful strategy for forgiveness, recognizing that forgiveness is not a static state, but rather a skill and a practice. We also discuss how optimism, hope, and gratitude nurture your well-being and shape what you pay attention to in life.

To stay focused on what really matters in life, you will probably want to make some changes in how you live today. How ready *are* you to make lasting change in your life? In chapter 6, we investigate why and how motivation for making changes waxes and wanes. We will describe how successful change actually happens (Prochaska et al. 1994) so that you can be well equipped to make lasting changes. You will be able to assess where your motivation is lacking. Then you can sharpen your focus through techniques like mindful meditation. Your level of motivation will then be matched with appropriate activities. We assure you that, regardless of where you are today, there are activities that will help you move toward staying focused on what really matters in your life.

YOUR HAPPINESS

We will define happiness in a minute but first let us look at how the general concept of happiness has been perceived. At one time, "happy" people were seen as not being bright or serious thinkers. Research has examined the "happy-but-dumb" connection (Seligman 2002). It appears that happy people actually make better life decisions. For example, they appear to be more health and safety conscious (and better able to endure pain) than people who are not happy. While research has shown that unhappy people may be more accurate when taking tests or preparing their income tax returns, happy people are more creative, generous, and tolerant. Clearly, we recognize that there are negative aspects of life, and a simple Pollyanna view is not the answer (Gable and Haidt 2005). So what is happiness?

Happiness is defined by a high degree of life satisfaction, frequent positive feelings, and infrequent negative feelings (Lyubomirsky et al 2005). Three factors contribute to our general, sustained level of happiness: genetics, circumstances, and intentional activity (Lyubomirsky et al 2005). Our genetic code is responsible for about 50 percent of our happiness level. Circumstances like gender, ethnicity, marital status, and health account for about 10 percent of our sustained happiness. It is the third category, intentional activities, which we focus on in this book. After all, these are the areas that we are most likely to be able to change. To increase our happiness and well-being, we can change in three areas: behavior, thoughts, and activities. At times, these categories overlap. We can adopt new behaviors (regular exercise, acts of kindness to others) thinking patterns (gratitude, optimism, and forgiveness), and other intentional activities (devoting time and energy to meaningful activity). We suggest a variety of these activities to you. We also encourage thoughtful self-reflection that is designed to enhance your level of happiness and well-being.

YOUR EXPECTATIONS

We believe that this book is unique in combining various topics and approaches. We think it's reasonable for you to expect to be guided to sharpen your focus as you identify and increase activities that are filled with meaning and purpose. You can also count on developing a clear statement of your spiritual practices, beliefs, and experiences. As you connect your spirituality with the activities of your daily life, you can begin to experience the benefits this application will bring to your physical and emotional health. By assessing your current motivation to make positive change, you can develop a personal focus plan to match your motivational level. The goal of staying focused on what matters to you is the central theme that unifies all the chapters in the book.

There are many approaches to reading this book. You may read quickly through all the chapters to get an overview, then return to complete the exercises that we suggest. Perhaps, you will just read a couple of chapters to get a feel for whether now is the right time for you to devote the energy to this book. Or you may start on page one and systematically work through the book to develop deeper insight into how you want to live your life. As we said, there are many approaches. Whatever fits for you now will be what you choose. Hopefully, you will have this book on hand for a while and will use it in the way that truly benefits you.

ARE YOU READY?

Before you begin working through this book, we suggest that you get a journal in which you may record responses and insights from the exercises. We suggest that you use your journal often as you move through the book. Thoughtful self-reflection can be beneficial. You gain what you give. If you give little effort, you may gain little. If, on the other hand, you treat the topic of your life's focus with the regard it deserves, your rewards will be greater.

You will reflect on questions raised by Emerson in the opening quote. What is meaningful to you? Are you living in accord with your values? Do you worship society's material trappings? Do you use your intuition to live a life that is right for you?

Time and attention are limited. They are precious commodities. It's important to know what to do during the brief period in which you are alive. While you are questioning, you're moving rapidly through life. As you proceed through these pages, we think that you will agree with Emerson: What you worship, you become. Your focus becomes your life.

Now, if you are ready, let's get started.

Chapter 1

Life in the Age of Distraction

Attention: Anyone who:

- ■ Watches television
- ■ Shops at the mall
- ■ Goes to the movies
- ■ Uses the Internet
- ■ Reads a newspaper
- ■ Glances at billboards
- ■ Listens to the radio
- ■ Browses through magazines

There is a battle being waged right now that most of us don't even realize. The weapons look innocuous, and the battlefield may be unnoticed. While no one will die in all of this, in a spiritual sense, lives are at stake. What you hold most dear is in danger of being lost. It doesn't need to be this way.

This book is about focusing your attention. We've found in our clinical work, and research has shown, that those who achieve happiness in their lives have the ability to focus on goals and values and live accordingly.

But you may have noticed that it's becoming increasingly difficult to maintain focus. Big business has succeeded in increasing its intrusion into our consciousness, even using the study of psychology to learn new methods to gain entrance. Because maintaining focus is crucial to happiness and satisfaction, it's important to take a look at how the culture we're living in works to defeat this focus and steal our attention. We'll begin by exploring just what we mean by this notion of "attention" and understanding how it can be manipulated.

THE STUDY OF ATTENTION

What is this psychological concept known as "attention"? Put most basically, it refers to the cognitive process of selectively concentrating on one thing while ignoring something else. A simple example is when you are talking with a friend at a restaurant. You are listening to your companion as you filter out the discussion at the next table. Of course, you can split attention and do so frequently, for example, when you drive your car while listening to the radio.

In 1890, E. W. Scripture, Ph.D., wrote *Thinking, Feeling, Doing.* Scripture stated in this early book that advertisers make it their business to know how to attract attention. The object of attention must be big, bright, or intense, arouse a feeling, create curiosity, and/or make a rapid change. For attention to be maintained, novelty is essential. Attention turns to inattention when we grow accustomed to something and cease to notice it.

Attention has been the subject of psychological study in this country from the mid 1800s. At that time the only method of looking at attention was introspection and self-report of experiences. It was not until the 1950s that the scientific method began to be applied to this topic. That is when what is called the *cognitive revolution* began. The cognitive revolution consisted of the study of thoughts, feelings, learning approaches, values, and beliefs, as well as behavior. Then, in the

1990s MRIs began to advance our understanding of what is happening in the brain during the various attentional processes

---

THE PROBLEM, AS WE SEE IT

Take a moment to consider how the technology of cell phones, the Internet, e-mail, WiFi, PDAs, and desktop publishing (to name just a few) has vastly increased the amount and variety of information that beckons to our attention each day. We are also faced with a greater number of options in virtually everything we do. These distractions steal the time and energy we need for actively seeking ways to find meaning in our lives. We are more likely to passively sit back and let others do that for us. Our so-called entertainment continues to become more graphically violent and sexually explicit. This is because that which was novel last year has become passé. In order to hold our attention, advertisers and media producers must keep upping the ante (Sacharin 2001). If this is what you focus on, it is certainly influencing who you are on some deep level. If you passively allow your life to be influenced by those who only wish to profit from capturing your attention, we believe you are at risk of losing hold of the reins of your moral, ethical, and spiritual life.

A Plethora of Choices

Life is really more complicated now than at any other time in history. Greater choice and wider access to information can be a good thing, but it more often adds a burden to simple tasks like shopping or catching up on the news. A trip to the mall for a pair of sneakers is a far more complex task than it used to be. Dozens of types of sneakers in hundreds of styles and fits face the shopper. Simply knowing your shoe size barely begins to narrow the field. One is left wondering, if he might have found a lower price and a "better" model in the next store. We may regret our decisions, thinking that we could have done better if only we had examined the options more completely. In his book, *The Paradox of Choice*, sociologist Barry Schwartz writes that the experience of all of these choices for the average person has the effect of increasing stress and depression and reducing overall satisfaction (2004).

In a later work, Schwartz suggests that older people are less likely to review all their choices (2005). They have learned, through experience, to live with what is good enough. Schwartz also believes that older people have learned that limited options have advantages. Certainly, having choices is essential for a sense of freedom in life. However, more choices do not automatically create happiness. Sometimes less is more.

An individual who wishes to focus on and live a deeply spiritual life faces a greater number of distractions than ever before in history. The distractions are now more sophisticated, too. What is this new age of seemingly infinite choice doing to us? It influences business leaders, the work life of employees, and the everyday life of each of us as individuals. We will consider this but first, let us put things into perspective.

So What Else Is New?

You may now be asking yourself, what is new here? Life has been hectic for years, right? Actually, it's never been like this before. The very reason corporations and advertisers are clamoring more and more frantically for our focus is because there has never been so much competition for our attention (Sacharin 2001). We live in a different world than we did even five years ago. The changes have come rapidly and are now an entrenched part of our culture. We, as a society, have become essentially numbed by all the information, novelty, and violence directed toward us. The average American now sees hundreds of advertisements each day. According to the United States Postal Service, American companies sent us 95 billion pieces of direct mail in 2004, up from 77 billion in 1997. This figure was projected to climb to 98.2 billion in 2005. Companies are using the Internet more effectively now, too. Web logs (called *blogs*), used by individuals as online journals, have been discovered by companies as an even more effective way to target market products to smaller niche groups. Before the Internet, e-mail, satellite television and radio, it was important for a company to just get a message out to customers. Now the unprecedented array of choices presents a unique new challenge to advertisers. There is *so* much information coming from all directions that, in order for advertisers to be successful, they are required to not only stand out and captivate our attention, but they must also learn how to keep it and manage it. For this reason, business academics tell us that we have gone beyond the Information Age; we have entered the "Attention Age" (Davenport and Beck 2001), where the consumer's attention is the commodity for which advertisers must compete with one another—and with us.

Costs and Benefits

In some ways this has been good for consumers. Because buyers have more options, sellers are forced to compete more than ever on various fronts, including how they price goods. Consumers have never had so many choices of good quality and inexpensive products.

Unfortunately, many consumers are also employees of companies that are affected negatively by this downward price pressure. As costs go down for goods, companies are under more pressure to cut production costs, which has meant workers are required to be more productive. Workers have never been responsible for so many tasks. It is now much more common than ever for both parents in households to work outside the home, and most full-time positions require far more than forty hours of work per week. Many professional and trade workers are seeing jobs in their sectors sent overseas. All of this means less free time, energy, and financial security for many.

COMPETITION FOR YOUR ATTENTION

What the corporate world wants, and spends millions trying to obtain, is our attention. *If our attention is so valuable, do we want to give it away?* As this book is being written, corporations are implementing new and more sophisticated ways to capture our attention, including giving us free access to information or entertainment they believe we will want. Advertisements are also being loaded into the entertainment we purchase. For example, a trip to the movies now includes not only coming attractions, but also advertisements for movie soundtracks, DVDs, apparel, and fast food.

Corporations spend millions of research dollars each year trying to learn how to better manage our attention and essentially own a piece of our minds. And they do a good job. Just look around. How many companies have managed to insert their brand names into our immediate surroundings? It has been increasingly difficult to buy a product that one wants and needs without also volunteering by default to advertise for the company brand. Have you noticed how difficult it is to buy clothing that does not double as a billboard for a corporation? Chances are our shirts, jeans, sneakers, hats, and even underwear come embossed with a company logo. It is no wonder that we are more familiar with our corporate leaders than with our leaders in government. More people can probably name the founder of Wal-Mart than the U.S. Secretary of State.

Through repetition, advertisers have inserted their products into our collective consciousness. A disturbing illustration of this is seen in Morgan Spurlock's 2004 film about the fast-food industry, *Super-Size Me*. In the film, Spurlock was dismayed that the image of Ronald McDonald was more recognizable to the third-grade students he met than pictures of George Washington or Jesus.

Awareness and Choice

We are not opposed to advertising and consumer research. After all, how else would we know about the products that enhance the quality of our lives? How would companies improve products to make them more useful to us? We simply think it is important to recognize the sophistication of the technology of attention management being used by companies to attempt to control a portion of our psychic energy. If we are not aware of this and do nothing about it, we end up with very little influence over where our precious daily allotment of concentration and focus is used. Consider how much focus is lost each day as we absorb unwanted information from radio, television, e-mail, billboards, magazines, and the Internet.

Distraction may be briefly defined as attention pulled away from that which is important. However, it is necessary to identify what is important before we can guard against distraction. In a world where there are so many competing forces for our attention, it can be difficult to know what to consider important. The difficulty is that "important" is a subjective term; its meaning depends largely upon whom you ask. What's important to you is not necessarily important to me. Consider for example the salesperson who is calling you at dinner time. This caller needs to close a certain number of sales each shift to keep her job. She is an individual with a life, bills, loved ones, and a need to earn a living. To that individual, speaking with you is very important. To you, however, this call is not important and is clearly a distraction from your life. In your dining room, with your family gathered around the table, a hot meal being served, the peace broken by a ringing phone lends an element of urgency to the atmosphere. Regardless of what you do, you have been distracted by this unimportant intrusion. If you allow your voice mail to intercept the call, you may then be distracted by thoughts about who called until you review the message. In a culture in which we are never really out of contact with the world, knowing that a message is waiting can be a pull too tempting to ignore.

Joseph Urgo writes in his book *In the Age of Distraction* that the quiet days of sitting alone with a book are being replaced by passive consumption of "information as entertainment," where we are inundated with reports of cheating spouses and small town murders (2000). The so-called information age has brought with it the electronic siren song of infinite possibilities realized by simply clicking a button. The result is that we are perpetually going somewhere at the price of never really *being* anywhere. We are being programmed to think that simply looking out a non-Microsoft window at nature, experiencing the here-and-now, may be a quaint waste of time. The real irony is that many people today report feeling rushed and believe that they have less time for such luxuries than prior generations—who did not have the benefit of all of the so-called time-saving devices (Urgo 2000).

Buying Happiness

It is a basic human desire to want to be happy. Many have been convinced through sophisticated advertising campaigns that happiness can be bought. It is a seductive myth, and it sells products. Actually, the greater the focus on material goods, the less sustained happiness and satisfaction are experienced by people (Bouen 2005).

At least since the time of Aristotle, 2300 years ago, humans have consciously sought happiness. Obviously, much has changed since then, but our search for a good quality of life has not. There is no shortage of commercial enterprises competing for our attention with the goal of convincing us to buy. At the heart of every successful advertising campaign is the basic notion that happiness can be bought and that the "good life" may be owned.

Although it may be hard to believe, financial status may not be a significant contributor to life satisfaction and happiness (Hong and Giannakopoulos 1995). Actually, it has been demonstrated that both lottery winners and recent paraplegics alike return to their baseline mood relatively soon after either event (Brickman et al. 1978). Neither financial windfall nor significant physical debilitation alone is capable of making a person more or less satisfied with life. Cognitive psycho-therapists have been telling us for years that it is not *what* happens to us, but how we *think* about what happens that really determines our level of contentment and happiness (Suh, Diener, and Fujita 1996). These ideas are far from new, but they are still relatively unknown or unacknowledged in our society at large. Messages like these are easily drowned out in a culture obsessed with selling us on youth, perfect health, and the accumulation of material possessions.

Paul Pearsall, a psychologist from Honolulu, incorporates ancient wisdom with modern research. He has identified that a significant number of people with "toxic success" crave more status, money, and responsibility. However, they do not have the energy and time to truly enjoy what they have. To solve this problem, these people do not need skills in time management. Rather, they need to learn attention management. The solution lies not in their schedule but in how they focus their attention (Chamberlin 2004).

LEARNING TO FOCUS

Certainly the most important task for an individual wishing to live a spiritual, meaningful, and happy life is focusing one's attention on living in accordance with a core set of values. So you see, it serves the interest of both individuals and corporations to master the art and science of attention management, a psychological term for the intentional focusing of attention. This is the heart of the struggle between what big business wants and what we truly need. Living a life focused on a set of values and ethical guidelines allows us to derive a deep sense of the meaning of life and our purpose in it. This can be attained by adopting a formal religion, establishing a set of spiritual beliefs and practices, or by clarifying secular values and ethics and living in accordance with them.

In our work as therapists we encounter individuals, not corpo-rations. These individuals tell us that they have no time to catch up anywhere in their lives. They report feeling estranged from themselves and their families. Many describe not living the life they had envisioned for themselves. They are discouraged, with little energy to try something new. We can understand this. But the problem is that doing nothing takes energy, too, and prevents deep satisfaction from emerging. Just as a garden filled with weeds is left with no nutrients or space to allow flowers to grow, a life filled with distraction does not allow the time or attention for what really matters in life.

When you wake up to your life in the deepest sense, possibilities emerge that you could not see before. We encourage you to go through this book as an act of faith in the idea that any realistic goal is possible to attain with the right tools and proper motivation, even if you can't imagine it right now.

The key to finding real happiness, as opposed to the temporary amusement of distraction, requires looking inward through some form of awareness or meditation and following a path to meaning. The journey requires attention and focus. The quest for deep happiness is only realized when you are able to sustain your attention and focus on what is important, valuable, and meaningful to you. We believe that this is the root of every spiritual tradition and also the key to learning how to focus on what really matters and tuning out what doesn't.

You can move forward equipped with skills to stop squandering your valuable focus. We truly believe that your focus does become your life.

Chapter 2

Staying Focused

Why should we live in such a hurry and waste of life?
We are determined to be starved before we are hungry.
I wish to live deliberately, to front only the essential facts of life.
I wish to learn what life has to teach, and not,
when I come to die, discover that I have not lived.

—Henry David Thoreau*

St. Benedict required *stabilitas loci* ("stable place") from the monks in his order (Sewald 2003). They promised to spend their lives in one

---

* Reprinted with permission of Random House, Inc.

monastery, to maintain a peaceful mind, and to be true to their chosen way of living. The monks didn't have to cope with moving from place to place nor make the decisions required by a life of physical and economic mobility. But you probably do.

Is it possible for you to live in the real world and be peaceful and true to yourself? In order to find peace and clarity in everyday life, do you need the phone to stop ringing and all demands for your attention to cease? This may seem ideal but not practical. Rather, it would be better to find strategies to maintain a clear and peaceful mind amid the hectic schedule that is your life.

How can you minimize distractions and overlook things that don't matter and distract you from your goals? How can you effectively manage your attention to focus on what is important to you? We will talk about these crucial questions in this chapter.

To focus means to concentrate attention or produce a clear image. Think about a camera lens. It consists of several lenses combined into one unit. We propose that the lens through which you see your life is also actually comprised of a number of lenses: your values, interests, passions, and daily responsibilities. With mindful attention, these lenses can converge into a single unit to produce a clear, sharp focus that is uniquely your own.

One of the most powerful ways to concentrate attention and sharpen your focus is to use mindfulness skills. Before we examine which skills may be the most helpful to you, let's review some of the basics. *Mindfulness* means awareness. It is an English word, but the Buddhist concept dates back many centuries. The concept of mindfulness, as used in our book, has no specific religious connection. Also, we will not be looking at mindfulness as an altered state of consciousness. Rather, we'll define the common processes we all use to pay attention.

Mindfulness is a psychological (and perhaps spiritual) awareness of what you are thinking and doing, a way of seeing things as they really are. Through mindfulness you can become aware of when you are stuck in a thought or behavior pattern. You can identify when you are distracted by competing stimuli that take you off track. Then, once aware, you have the power to choose to redirect your focus, guided by your values and priorities. Mindfulness is a particular way of paying attention so that you may enhance the quality of your life. For that reason, mindfulness strategies are given considerable emphasis in our book.

MINDLESSNESS

Ellen Langer, a psychologist and researcher, has spent most of her professional career investigating the concepts of mindfulness, but she began her research by investigating the lack of awareness she calls *mindlessness*. From her experiments with mindlessness, she developed her understanding of what is involved in paying attention mindfully (Langer 1989).

We have all had the experience of mindlessness, of operating on automatic pilot. Did you ever eat dinner in front of the television and finish your meal without being aware of how the food tasted or how much you ate—or even what you ate? Have you asked for directions but not listened when they were given? When introduced to a stranger, do you hear his name then immediately forget it? There are countless times during the day when we switch to automatic pilot. Some say that being on automatic pilot for some tasks is good. It allows you to have energy to focus on more important things. When do you use automatic pilot? Do you think you would like to shift some of those tasks into more mindful attention?

In the preceding chapter we talked about the hundreds, if not thousands, of daily messages we receive as a result of someone's attempt to direct our thoughts, feelings, and behavior. When we are distracted by too many choices, fatigue and confusion can set in. We get overwhelmed. We may automatically tune out the overstimulation and become mindless.

Mindlessness can also come from repetition. Think about the long monotonous highway that hypnotizes you. You may arrive at your destination with little memory of how you got there. How many times did you mindlessly say the Pledge of Allegiance in school? Most of us repeated it so often that we didn't even know what we were saying. If we want to be present in our lives and make choices about things that are truly important to us, then we have to pay attention as if it really matters. Because it does.

MINDFULNESS

The opposite of mindlessness is mindfulness. Mindfulness means to pay attention as if it *really* matters. It is being present in the moment and fully aware. You don't need to be a Buddhist to meditate. Anyone can do it. A common misunderstanding is that meditation or prayer is a special state of relaxation or a slowing down of the mind. Actually it can also be a state of keen awareness in any circumstance or situation. Mindfulness means looking deeply into the present. This can be done by anyone, anywhere, at any time. Mindfulness is a choice we make.

Mindful awareness can be developed by meditation or contemplative prayer. The practice of mindfulness is not reserved for the meditation cushion or the church pew. It is a cognitive process that helps us pay attention to our thoughts and feelings in the present moment. Any experience of breathing, sitting, walking, seeing, hearing, tasting, smelling, or touching can be a meditation in mindfulness. Examples of various mindful meditation practices are included later in this chapter.

Mindfulness-based stress reduction (MBSR) is a specific application of mindfulness practices. It was developed from Jon Kabat-Zinn's research. Over 1,000 studies based on MBSR are now in print (Whylie and Simon 2004). Kabat-Zinn has been able to combine eastern traditions and western science in mind-body medicine. He has clearly demonstrated the value of mindful awareness in the process of healing. His techniques have been taught to 16,000 patients and 5,000 medical professionals (Whylie and Simon 2004). MBSR has been shown to reduce chronic pain, high blood pressure, cholesterol levels, depression, anxiety, posttraumatic stress disorder, and eating disorders. This set of mindfulness practices can alter immune responses to influenza vaccine and affect how emotions are regulated in the brain. Even people with psoriasis, a chronic skin condition, heal faster when they meditate during their light box treatments. Research continues on the impact of MBSR on conditions such as irritable bowel syndrome, prostate cancer, fibromyalgia, and chronic fatigue syndrome.

Barriers to Mindfulness

As the wise Hebrew scholars warn us in the Talmud, we do not see things as they are. We see things as we are (Lesser 1999). Elizabeth Lesser, cofounder of the Omega Institute in Rhinebeck, New York, encourages us to be aware of how our "false ego" may present barriers to mindfulness. While the concept of ego has many definitions, she suggests that we see our ego simply as a form of gravity that holds our concept of self together. When its force is too strong, we feel self-important. When its force is too weak, we feel helpless and afraid. Both extremes are out of balance. Getting rid of the ego (as if that were possible) is not the answer. Rather, approaching our imbalance with compassion and understanding is key. It is better to be familiar with the ego and recognize when it serves and when it acts to our detriment.

When our minds become filled with negative thoughts towards others or ourselves, we are dealing with a false ego—one extreme or the other. Lesser identifies four barriers used by the ego to preserve the status quo so that we stay either helpless and afraid or self-centered and self-important (1999). Those barriers are pain, sleepiness, restlessness, and judgment. Gently working with these parts of our life is important.

If pain keeps us from mindful meditation, it is important not to judge ourselves or the pain. Being critical of our pain only tends to intensify it. Lesser suggests we pay "bare attention" which, in this case, means to separate the pain from our reactions to the pain. Working with our pain and learning to separate our pain from our reactions and judgments will help keep us from being distracted.

When we are restless or sleepy, it may be difficult to maintain a mindful focus. Sometimes it helps to stretch and breathe deeply to refocus our attention. Again, we recognize that our thoughts, feelings, and judgments about our restlessness or sleepiness are just that— thoughts, feelings, and judgments about our physical sensations. Our harsh judgments of ourselves and of our experiences need to be acknowledged and gently embraced. It is an amazing paradox that by accepting parts of ourselves that are unappealing to us, those parts seem to be transformed, and we can go on without those barriers to mindfulness. Now let us look at what skills are involved in mindful practice.

Skills for Mindfulness

Jon Kabat-Zinn wrote about the foundations of mindful practice (1990). First, it is helpful to learn to be an impartial witness to your own internal and external experiences in a nonjudgmental manner. As you develop your patience, you recognize that everything unfolds in its own time. Staying in the present moment, you learn to accept things as they really are and begin to trust your own experience.

When you are mindfully aware, you are able to be fully present and see the full range of experiences that exist on a moment-to-moment basis. Most of us don't spend our days living totally in the present. We think of the past and dwell on what happened yesterday or we think about dreams or fears about tomorrow. In addition to dwelling on the past or projecting into the future, we are affected by our cognitive filters of opinion and judgment.

In developing mindfulness, an important skill to acquire is the awareness of an *observing self* so that you can simply be aware of your experience without judging it. It is as if you become an impartial witness while still functioning in the here and now. Anthropologists coined the term *participant observer* to describe what it is like to be introspective while engaged in the activities of an exotic culture (Levine 2000). You do not have to be observing a tribal ceremony in a distant land to be a participant observer or observing self. You can learn to become a participant observer in your own life through mindfully observing your experiences as they happen.

Mindful meditation does not mean withdrawing from your life. Quite the opposite! It facilitates more total involvement in your experience. You can be fully present in your life and notice what is happening inside you and around you without necessarily trying to change it. You can learn to step back from your experience without feeling a need to judge it. When you're mindfully aware, you have the attitude of acceptance without being compelled to judge everything as good or bad. You can simply notice more clearly what is happening.

For instance, through your observing self, you recognize that your thoughts and feelings are just that—thoughts and feelings. They are transient. They come and go rather quickly if you don't get stuck on them. Thoughts and feelings are not actions. They are a natural part of being alive. They do not define you as a person, nor do they necessarily require action on your part.

What is happening internally and what is occurring in the environment? Determining this necessitates some objectivity. For example, when a feeling of fear arises, most people jump to the notion that something bad will happen. Psychologist Marsha Linehan describes the importance of developing the skill to describe the experience in words (1993). With increased objective awareness and description, you recognize that feeling afraid does not automatically mean something bad will happen. The internal feeling of fear and the external event are two distinct experiences. When they are recognized as separate, you'll be less likely to jump into an emotionally motivated reaction. If you need to take action based on an external event, you may do so. But your tendency to leap into action based solely on panic can be substantially reduced with awareness of the distinction between internal and external events.

Can we be mindful all the time? Probably not. But it is possible to be alert and focused for many of our waking hours. Researcher E. J. Langer helps us understand how to do this with a metaphor about the CEO of a large corporation. The CEO pays attention to the big picture of how the corporation functions but does not attend to every small detail of functioning. The effective CEO chooses when and where to be mindful. A mindful CEO develops the skill of an observing self to be mindful of her own thoughts and performance. The CEOs observing self helps her stay focused on the big picture and not drift into mindlessness (1989).

Soft Vigilance

If you want to know yourself, you must observe and recognize what goes on in your mind (Nhat Hanh 1975). This is best accomplished by *soft vigilance*, a term used by Langer to describe mindful attention (1997). Soft vigilance is not the same as *hypervigilance*, an intense and static focus that requires great effort and cannot be sustained for long periods. Rather, soft vigilance is energizing and enjoyable. It permits novelty so we can maintain interest for extended periods of time. Mindfulness provides all this: sustained focus with novelty, increased energy, and relatively little effort. Try some of these exercises in mindful attention and see for yourself.

Mindful Breathing

A mindful breathing meditation is a very effective strategy, not just to soothe yourself but to sharpen your awareness. Whenever your thoughts are scattered, use your breath to take hold of your focus. Use your breath to stop distractions and build concentration.

Breathing can be very enjoyable, especially when the air is clean and your nose and lungs are clear. Your key to mindful attention is as close as your breath. Pay attention to your own breathing at this minute.

When you inhale, do you raise your chest? Do you drop your chest as you exhale? Have you ever watched a baby breathe? Notice that her tummy, rather than her chest, rises when she inhales and becomes flat when she exhales. This is called diaphragmatic breathing, and it came naturally to all of us as babies. This is the opposite of how most of us breathe today. As we get older we carry tension in our bodies and don't relax our stomachs as we did when we were babies. It is much more efficient and effective to breathe "naturally." So let's start practicing.

It is important when you exhale to empty most of the air from your lungs. Then you are ready for a fresh supply of oxygen. When you don't do this efficiently, carbon dioxide builds up in your bloodstream. This makes you nervous and causes anxiety. When you feel anxious it is natural to take rapid, shallow breaths, and this makes you even more anxious. You must empty your lungs of the old, carbon dioxide–filled air. Then you can inhale fresh air and get enough oxygen to your brain. So let's see how it's done.

The steps are simple. It is useful to start out doing this while lying on your back so you can watch your chest or stomach. Begin by placing your hands on the lower edge of your rib cage. This is where your diaphragm, a large umbrella-shaped muscle, is attached. As you exhale, pull in your stomach so that the air is forced out from the bottom of your lungs. Do this slowly for a count of four. Now hold your breath for a count of two.

Now, inhale slowly, for a count of four, expanding your stomach as you do. Hold for a count of two, then slowly exhale for a count of four as you repeat the process in the previous paragraph.

Repeat this cycle three times. Remember to inhale or exhale for a count of four, hold for two, then exhale or inhale for four. This is called "4-2-4" breathing. Do this slowly and mindfully. Your brain gets more oxygen as you become calm and more focused. You may want to practice diaphragmatic breathing like this, counting while you breathe, several times a day.

When you have practiced breathing deeply and slowly for about a month, you may stop counting 4-2-4 and simply say the words "breathing in" and "breathing out" or "in breath" and "out breath." After a month's time you will be used to the natural rhythm since the 4-2-4 count has guided your pace.

Every breath has three parts: the in-breath, the pause, the out-breath. There is a natural rhythm to the process of the active part, the pause, and the passive part. Some people who practice yoga believe that we should use our breath wisely and economically since they believe we have only a finite number of breaths between birth and death (Sewald 2003).

You may practice mindful breathing either in formal or informal practice (Kabat-Zinn 1990). The formal discipline requires that you set aside a particular time and assume a special posture. During this time of diaphragmatic breathing, you focus on the in breath and the out breath. Remember, you don't have to count 4-2-4 after you are accustomed to the slow pace of the breathing cycle. Simply focus on breathing in and breathing out. Take the time to create the ritual, because meditating this way can calm and renew you.

Or you may prefer an informal approach. Just pause throughout your day, bring yourself to the present moment, and focus on your breathing. While this can be as valuable as formal meditative practice, it is easy to forget to pause for these moments of mindful breathing.

When you notice thoughts intruding on your meditation, don't judge yourself or your thoughts. Avoid saying "I shouldn't be having this thought," or "I'm not meditating the right way." Just acknowledge that you are having a thought and return your attention to your breathing. When thoughts enter, just let them come and go in an effortless way and return your awareness to your breathing. The focus on your breathing isn't just a way to avoid the distractions of your thoughts and feelings. It is a vehicle to connect your mind and body and to "open the gate of wisdom" (Thich Nhat Hanh 1975).

Our minds shift focus from minute to minute. When life gets chaotic and we get distracted, focusing on our breath can help us change channels and direct our awareness where we want it to go. Kabat-Zinn believes that mindfulness is a way to wake up to the best part of ourselves. We can wake up to who we really are—to the deepest and sometimes undeveloped parts of ourselves (Whylie & Simon 1994).

A little later, we will suggest reminders for you to use so that you can remember to do this type of breathing at helpful intervals throughout the day. But now let's turn to other mindful practices that can center you and sharpen your focus.

Mindful Walking

Try mindful walking. Begin by focusing your attention on your breathing and take a few slow, deep breaths. Now take off your shoes and socks and stand up. As you stand in your bare feet, take one or two very slow and deliberate steps forward. Notice that your heel touches the ground first, then your foot rolls down to meet the ground with your toes touching last. Focus on how that feels. This is the first step (no pun intended) in mindful walking. Be aware of the present moment as you walk. Distractions fade from your mind as you bring your total attention to the place when your foot touches the ground.

As you might imagine, there are many variations on this theme. It's one thing to practice this meditation in your living room or back yard. It's quite another to walk this slowly in public. It may seem strange to walk at this slow pace. So when you are walking in public, walk at your normal speed, but mindfully notice something else about your experience. Pay attention to the temperature of the air as it touches your face. Notice the regular rhythm of your breath. Focus on the objects you pass—their shape, size, and texture. Appreciate how it feels to have some control over your thoughts and focus. You'll want to develop this focusing skill in a number of settings.

Mindful Sitting

If you wanted to meditate while sitting in an upright, dignified position for an extended period, you may choose to sit on the floor. It would be important to keep your body erect but not stiff. Your posture would show a wakefulness, even if your eyes are closed (Kabat-Zinn 1994).

However, you could also just sit comfortably in a chair for the purpose of this exercise. Close your eyes, take a few deep breaths, then change position in your chair and notice how your muscles respond as you shift your weight. Slowly rub the fingers of one hand on the palm of your other hand, and notice those sensations. Now, gently flex, then relax, each arm and leg. Feel the difference between the tension and the relaxation. Notice how the chair supports your back and legs. If you can lean your head back into the chair, take a few deep breaths and appreciate how little effort it takes to remain in that position.

Mindful Seeing

For a visual meditation, begin by focusing on your breathing as you take a few slow, deep breaths. Raise your eyes from this page and slowly look around the room. Start by looking around the floor, from left to right, until you have seen every part of the room's floor. Then slowly scan the rest of the room. Notice the light, the shapes of the furniture, the colors in the carpet, etc.

What types of visual experiences do you typically find soothing and engaging? Take several deep, mindful breaths and experiment. Pick an object from the table and really look at it. Pay attention to it as if it really matters. Look at a flower or the face of a loved one. Light a candle and watch the flame. Look at a painting or a photograph. Pay attention to something beautiful in nature. Watch fish swim in an aquarium.

Mindful Hearing

To have an experience in mindful hearing, begin with a few deep, slow breaths. In the room in which you're sitting, stop reading and just listen. What do you hear? As you take a few deep breaths, listen to the sound of your inhalation and your exhalation.

Is there particular music you play to match your mood? If you want to change the way you are feeling, what do you listen to? Is it music or sounds from nature that help bring you into the present? Does the breathing of a sleeping pet or loved one soothe and calm you? Get to know what auditory stimulation suits you and enhances your ability to stay in the moment.

Mindful Smelling

Olfactory experiences can be very powerful, and you can benefit from this power by focusing mindfully on your sense of smell. Close your eyes and take a few deep breaths. See if you can identify any immediate scents. Experiment. What are your favorites? Do you enjoy the fragrance of flowers, pine, scented candles? Learn to associate certain scents with slow, mindful breathing. Appreciate how wonderful it is to breathe and be alive.

Mindful Tasting

Before you begin a meditation in taste, take a few mindful breaths to help center yourself. Then put a raisin or another small piece of fruit in your mouth. Do not chew it. Just let it stay on your tongue and notice how it feels against the roof of your mouth. Can you taste anything? Does the sweetness start to become obvious? Then begin to slowly chew the raisin, noticing the taste and consistency.

You may use these mindful strategies while eating any of your meals. It is a unique experience to eat quietly and mindfully, noticing the taste and texture of your food. Please try this at least once. It can be a powerful experience.

Mindful Touching

There are many pleasant tactile sensations. A meditation in touch can be soothing or energizing. Close your eyes, take a few slow, deep breaths, and feel the texture of your chair with your hand. Repeat this several times with varying degrees of pressure. Does the texture feel different when you press down harder or softer? Rub your fingers over the smooth cover of this book. Is it cool to the touch? Touch something on a nearby table. Pay attention to the sensations, as if they really matter.

The next time you take a warm shower, notice how the water feels when it first touches your skin. Be aware of the texture of the shampoo or soap and how that transforms the feel of your hair and skin.

Enjoy the feel of clean sheets when you get into bed. Notice how your pillow compresses as you lay your head on it. Experience the softness of the blanket or other covering.

Meditation for All the Senses

Meditation is the act of bringing your conscious awareness to something. Mindfully focusing on one thing at a time helps reduce stress caused by preoccupations and obsessions. In mindful meditation, you practice becoming self-aware. You develop a fuller experience of being in your body and a clearer focus on your thoughts and feelings.

You have now experienced bringing yourself into the present while breathing, walking, sitting, eating, and performing some daily activities. You have more control than you realize over where your attention goes. Remember to practice exercising that control. You can tune into a sight, sound, smell, taste, touch, thought, or emotion at a second's notice. You do not need a fancy routine or mystical mantra. Just experiment and enjoy yourself. If you read *Coming to Our Senses: Healing Ourselves and the World Through Mindfulness* (2005) by Jon Kabat-Zinn, you will find helpful descriptions of how to tune your senses as you would tune an instrument. You will be able to increase the clarity, sensitivity, and range of your senses. We encourage you to explore this further.

A Day of Mindfulness

While it would be wonderful to spend every hour or every day in total mindfulness, it's not a practical goal for most of us. However, for the purpose of recognizing the value of mindfulness, it may be possible to set aside one day a week to devote yourself to mindful awareness. Perhaps you could choose Saturday as the day. Thich Nhat Hanh has some suggestions on how to do this, below (1975).

In your bedroom, place a reminder to be mindful. Place it where you will see it when you first awaken—on your dresser or ceiling. Then, when you see the reminder, you will focus on your breathing and pay close attention to how your muscles move as you get out of bed. You will be aware of how it feels to brush your teeth, take a shower, and prepare to eat your breakfast. Go through all the activities of the day with a focus on being present in the moment with everything you do or say. Of course, you may speak and interact with others, but notice that you are likely to lose your focus unless your awareness is well-practiced. As you return to your bed at the end of the day, follow your breath in mindfulness until you ease into sleep.

You may not have an entire day every week to practice this. But we encourage you to periodically block out several hours of time to practice the variety of meditations suggested in this chapter.

Mindfulness with a Half-Smile

Thich Nhat Hanh also suggests exercises with a half-smile (1975). Take several deep, mindful breaths and allow a half-smile to appear on your face. You may want to hang a sign as a reminder for you to smile as you go through your mindful meditation practices. Practice the half-smile while walking, standing, sitting, listening to music, etc. Even when you have an irritating thought, take a few deep, slow breaths and maintain a half-smile as you do. Notice the result. What might it be? A lightening of sorts?

Creative Silence

Thomas Merton wrote about the many dimensions of silence (1979). Through reflection, sitting in silence can help us synthesize and integrate thoughts, feelings, and behavior. Silence allows us to focus our scattered energies. Otherwise, we may mindlessly "float along in the general noise" (40).

Merton believes that, for Christians, silent meditation has an even deeper motive. It permits the meditator to listen to God. In Merton's view, refusing to be open to the depth of silence is equivalent to refusing to connect to the God within. The belief is that sitting in silence allows an awareness to emerge of the value of the individual's existence and provides guidance for how to face the commitments of daily life. Further, the meditator develops an understanding of God's intention for them.

Silent meditation is important in many religions, including Hinduism, Buddhism, Judaism, and Christianity. Quakers listen quietly in community for the "inner moving of the Spirit" (Merton 1979). Secular interest in mindful meditation is widespread, as evidenced by the scientific research of meditation practice applied to mind-body healing. Regardless of theoretical underpinnings, selective attention through controlled focus has great value. Staying focused in the age of distraction is possible through a variety of mindful strategies.

Mindfulness and Creativity

Mindfulness has much in common with creativity. Instead of being stuck with an old mindset, mindfulness calls for openness to new information, awareness of more than one perspective, and creation of new mindsets (Langer 1989). In the previous exercises, you developed a different awareness than you may have had before, when you were operating on automatic pilot. When we are creative and mindful, we are more focused on the process of the moment than on the outcome.

Years ago, one of the authors was scheduled to give a lecture to a large group using slides that showed detailed graphs. It was at the end of the day, and most conference participants were tired of sitting and listening to presentations. Suddenly, the electricity went off at the conference center due to a storm, and the emergency generator could not provide all the power that was needed. Creative thinking was necessary to capture and maintain the participants' interest. The conference-center staff brought candles into the lecture room. The candlelight transformed the room. The lecture changed from a high-tech presentation to a more intimate discussion of the material. It was a chance for all participants, including the presenter, to be flexible, mindful, and open to a novel situation. Since reprints of the lecture and graphs were available to the audience, no crucial information was lost. No doubt that evening in the conference center was more memorable than a standard lecture format would have been.

RE-FOCUSING STRATEGIES

Chapter 1 explained how overloaded we are in this age of distraction. We think you will agree that the challenge is not to stretch even further to take in more information but, rather, to be mindful and discriminating about where our attention is focused. How can we minimize distractions and overlook things that don't matter? We all know what it's like to try to pay attention to something when we are distracted by something else. Suppose we are feeling emotional pain, and we don't want to focus on the negative. We can direct ourselves away from unpleasant thoughts and feelings. We can do this by mindfully attending to our breathing and being in the present moment. The additional strategies below can also help.

Thought Stopping

Thought stopping is a technique we recommend to clients and use ourselves. It is a simple, straightforward way to stop an annoying or distracting thought. Simply say "stop" to the thought. Then shift your focus by counting to ten, counting the colors in the rug on the floor, noticing the shadows cast by the lamp, etc. It's simple to do: say "stop," then shift your focus. It doesn't have to be any more complicated than that, but it will take practice on your part.

Changing the Setting

An obvious way to minimize distractions is to change the setting. For instance, turn off the television or the computer so you can bring your attention more fully to an activity you determine to be worthwhile (more about that in the next chapter).

Stop for a minute and honestly answer the question: How many hours each evening or weekend do you spend watching television or using the computer? Are you willing to cut that time in half to pay attention to something more meaningful to you?

If you are distracted by noise or commotion at work or at home, do you use earplugs or headphones if it's practical to do so? This is another way to cut down on distractions and give your focusing skills some practice.

What about your workplace clutter? Do you have materials for several projects out at the same time? It helps to put materials away when you're finished with a project. This seems obvious, but most of us grow accustomed to clutter. This often results in distraction.

Shifting Activities

When you are absorbed in unproductive, distressing, negative thoughts, simply change activities. If you're reading or watching television, get up and go for a walk. Try a brief exercise routine. Call a friend. Balance your checkbook. There are many things you can do. Just do something different. Often this is enough to shift your focus.

Adopting an Attitude of Gratitude

It's nearly impossible to be stuck in negative thoughts if you make a list of things for which you're grateful. There is more about this in following chapters, but for now it's sufficient to say that an attitude of gratitude goes a long way in distracting from unwanted thoughts. Just start making a list of simple things you appreciate, for example: a comfortable chair to sit in, warm boots on a cold day, a solid roof over your head, a refreshing drink when you are thirsty.

Making a Contribution

A great way to distract from your troubles and worries is to contribute time and energy to someone else. Again, we'll talk more about this later. We just want you to begin thinking about this helpful strategy for distracting from unwanted preoccupations.

Feeling Opposite Emotions

You can distract from any thought or emotion by intentionally engaging opposite emotions. One way to do this is by listening to certain kinds of music. You can read. You can dance. What works for you when you want to energize yourself because you are low? What calms you down when you feel nervous or agitated?

Thinking Other Thoughts

Sometimes, distracting yourself is as easy as counting to ten. Take a few deep breaths, then count to ten. If you are still obsessed by a thought, count backwards from fifty or from seventy-five or count to ninety-nine by threes. It doesn't really matter what formula you use. The point is to become familiar with what works for you. Stopping your preoccupations and switching channels to another thought can leave you free to mindfully engage yourself in something worthwhile. (In the next few chapters you'll determine what is truly worthy of your attention.)

Using Containment Strategies

If you've done what you can for the moment about a problem yet you continue to focus on it, there are ways to psychologically contain the problem that might be helpful. For example, close your eyes and picture building an imaginary wall between you and the problem. Or write the problem on a piece of paper and close it away in a container (envelope, drawer, box, etc.). As simple as this sounds, containment strategies can actually reduce your level of obsession as you redirect your focus and mindfully pursue another thought or task.

Finally, if you find that no other technique works for you, set aside a specific time to worry about the problem—but do it in a controlled way. Set the timer for ten minutes. Worry about the problem with no other thoughts in mind. When the timer rings to indicate the end of the ten minutes, get up and shift your activities. (Note: Do not start this right before bed or it will be difficult to get to sleep).

A PERSONAL EXPERIENCE WITH CONTAINMENT

One of our friends had a successful experience with a containment strategy. We hope that sharing this with you will give you ideas of how to creatively use the strategies we propose so that you can tune out the thoughts that are not helpful and truly don't matter. This is how our friend described her experience:

> When I stopped smoking in 1987, I became depressed and was distracted by many negative obsessions. It was hard to dispense with these thoughts and focus on more important matters.
> I was in a 12-step program to stop smoking at the time, hearing slogans and ideas from the other people in the program. I was advised to turn my worries over to a higher power, but this was difficult for me. I was told that I am expected to do what I can to solve a problem but, after I do that, I need to turn the outcome over to a higher power. I understood that I am responsible for my part of the problem-solving process, and I recognized that I could not control the outcome of my efforts. But the concept of turning things over to a higher power was

too abstract for me. I needed a more concrete strategy—and I found one. I took a brown lunch bag and wrote the initials G.O.D. on the side of the bag. I couldn't relate to a god in heaven, but I could accept the acronym of G.O.D. for Good Orderly Direction (since I agree that I am responsible for the footwork of solving my problems, even though I can't control the outcome). I was willing to write the problem on a slip of paper, date it, and put it into the G.O.D. bag. For example, one day I scribbled "Ruby's college tuition payment: 8/1/92" on a scrap of paper and dropped it into the bag. I continued to work and save for Ruby's tuition but I stopped obsessing about whether I would have enough money by the August deadline.

I was amazed that after I put each problem in the containment of the bag, I could stop obsessing about the outcome. My worries were always worse when I went to bed at night. The worries would just start spinning in my mind. I found that if I got up, wrote the problem on a slip of paper, dated it, and put it in the G.O.D. bag, I could fall asleep with no difficulty. This ritual has been helpful to me for many years. I keep all the little pieces of paper in the bag and every time I open the bag to deposit a new worry, I take out a few of the papers I had previously put in the bag. I review those worries that loomed so large at the time and marvel at how well those problems worked out. It helps to build my faith that I am responsible for the footwork in my life but that the outcome is not up to me. I have contained hundreds of worries since 1987 and have been able to free-up the physical, emotional, and spiritual energy that I need to focus on what I can change and on what really matters in my life.

JOURNALING

Psychologists have researched many techniques for helping people change behavior. The process of self-monitoring appears to be an effective strategy. It helps us to become aware of what we're thinking and feeling. It aids our objective self in developing insight.

Not only can journaling help you develop insight, it can build motivation to stay on track. Further, it is helpful to review your progress from time to time since it is reinforcing to see how far you have come. Journaling allows you to do this.

Have you ever used self-monitoring to develop insight and make changes? Think about this for a moment. Did you ever write down what you ate when you wanted to lose weight? Have you ever recorded your spending when you wanted to know where all your money goes? Have you ever kept a diary of your thoughts and feelings during times of difficulty?

Generally, people don't use the term self-monitoring. Rather, they say they keep a journal or write notes in some other way. We recommend that clients keep a journal while they are in therapy. We have kept journals ourselves from time to time.

If you have not already done so, please buy a notebook today or tomorrow. Use it as part of your process as you read through this book. You will receive more insight and benefit if you do. You will also be more likely to strengthen your motivation to stay on your path so that this book can make a lasting difference for you. You want to increase your ability to stay focused in this age of distraction. You are motivated to increase the level of meaning and purpose in your life. And journaling is simple (though not easy) to do. Please help yourself by keeping a journal and using it often for thoughtful self-reflection.

Before you proceed to the next section, take some time to review the section on mindful breathing and repeat the exercises that appealed to you (walking, sitting, eating, etc.). Write about your experiences in your journal. Remember that novelty is an important component in mindfulness, so keep your mindful practices fresh by varying them from time to time.

Next, review the section on refocusing strategies. Make a list of the ones that you're willing to try. Keep notes in your journal of what works for you. We suggest you do this so it's available for you to review as you complete the exercises in the book.

REMINDERS

It's one thing to read about focusing strategies and record the ones that work for you. It's quite another to remember to *use* the strategies when you need them. What might be good reminders for you to practice mindfulness in your daily activities?

Some people stop and pray when they hear church bells. In certain monasteries, when the bell rings, everyone stops what they are doing and prays or contemplates in a mindful way. They become present in the moment, and the quality of their experience improves. In Plum Village, a community established by Thich Nhat Hanh, a bell calls everyone to stop what they are doing and follow their breath. These reminders help the participants resist getting caught up in the pace of life and losing focus on what is truly important to them (Thich Nhat Hanh 1987). A minister we know uses the ring of the telephone to stop himself and shift his focus so he can answer the phone with a mindful attitude. We find it helpful to use a note or symbol to trigger an awareness to be mindful.

By now, you have practiced some of the mindful activities suggested in the chapter. You know which ones are particularly effective for you. Remind yourself to use those strategies. For example, to remind yourself to use mindful breathing, place a Post-It note in your work area to trigger your awareness of your breathing. Just write the word "Breathe" and place the note where you will see it often. If you tend to operate on automatic pilot, post a note that says "Notice what you're thinking." Or the note can simply say "Notice." What notes or symbols would be most effective for you?

Perhaps you would like to wear a different piece of jewelry or place your watch on your other arm. This will trigger recognition that something is different, and you will recall that you are to practice a mindfulness strategy. What will work for you? What can you change in your immediate environment to remind you to be mindful? Think about this. Follow through with constructing some reminders to trigger your awareness for more mindful participation in your life. Pay attention as if it really matters. Remember that your focus becomes your life.

Chapter 3

What Matters:
Meaningful Activity

*The place God calls you to is the place where your
deep gladness and the world's deep hunger meet.*

—Frederick Buechner*

Human beings are the only species who seek to attribute meaning to
their experiences. The concept of "what matters in life" may sound
vague and amorphous. But if we use goals to define what matters then
we have a way to measure what is meaningful to us. Of course, all goals

---

* Reprinted by permission of HarperCollins

aren't created equal. Striving for some goals can contribute to life satisfaction and well-being, while pursuing other goals can lead to dissatisfaction and problems.

POSITIVE PSYCHOLOGY

Many of us would say that to be happy is an important goal. Happiness is a by-product of being engaged in goals or activities that give your life a sense of meaning and purpose (Frankl 1959). Corey Keyes is a social psychologist and Jonathan Haidt is a social and cultural psychologist. They are experts in the area of positive psychology. These are the four main categories of goals proposed by Keyes and Haidt (2003):

1. Work and achievement goals address how committed you are to your work. Does it seem meaningful to you and others? Is it challenging to you?

2. Intimacy and relationships goals address how you relate to others. Do you trust them? Are you helpful to others, and do you let them know you care? Are you a good listener?

3. Religion and spirituality goals address your relationship to something greater than yourself. Do you have a higher power? Are you part of a faith community?

4. Finally, there are transcendence and generativity goals. Generativity means production to bring into existence. Is it important to you to transcend your own interests and contribute something to others, particularly younger people? Are you a good role model? Do you have concern and a commitment to future generations?

Goals in the areas of intimacy, spirituality, and generativity are typically connected with the positive feelings of what matters and is meaningful in life. On the other hand, there is a dark side to the emphasis on goals related to fame and fortune. People who strive to gain power and influence over others and achieve social recognition, financial success, and physical attractiveness are more likely to experience characteristics of narcissism, anxiety, depression, and physical illness (Kasser and Ryan 1996). Research has demonstrated that income is only moderately related to feelings of happiness and well-being (Myers 2000). Neglecting goals in the area of fulfilling relationships can lead to psychological and interpersonal problems (Kasser and Ryan 1996).

So far in this book, we have established that we live in the age of distraction, with many forces competing for our attention. We have started to become more mindful of how we can direct our attention where *we* want it to go. Now we are beginning to explore what truly matters and what is worthy of our focus. Before we go further, let's look more closely at what positive psychology, a relatively new area of psychology, has to offer us.

A Bit of History

Before World War II, there were three broad areas in psychology (Seligman 2002). The first area was the diagnosis and treatment of mental disorders. The second area focused on making work more productive and fulfilling through the development of industrial psychology. The third area studied how to develop genius and talent.

After World War II, the field of psychology became more narrowly defined. The National Institute of Mental Health (NIMH) was funded. This event narrowed the primary focus of psychology into the diagnosis and treatment of mental disorders. Through this emphasis, we have learned much about treating mental illness but we have learned little about how to prevent mental illness or how to strengthen the person's resiliency and improve the general quality of life. That is where positive psychology comes into the picture.

In 1995, Martin Seligman and his colleagues investigated how to teach skills to children and adults to help them prevent mental illness. They demonstrated that building on a person's strengths (such as hope, courage, and optimism) can actually serve as a buffer to depression and other disorders. Instead of focusing on what is wrong and weak, positive psychology focuses on what is right and strong. In chapter 5 we'll look further at positive-psychology research in the areas of quality of life, forgiveness, optimism, hope, and gratitude. Each of these areas is worthy of our focus and contributes to our happiness and well-being.

MEANINGFUL ACTIVITY

In this chapter you will concentrate on your strengths and interests and begin to develop your plan for increasing meaningful activity in your life. You have strengths and natural resiliencies that may have been present since childhood. By exploring your talents and strengths and connecting them to your priorities and spiritual beliefs, you can discern what gives your life a sense of meaning and purpose. We define *life purpose* to mean the very nature of your being. Your life's purpose lies at your core. Just as an acorn contains the knowledge and blueprint for the tree, your life's purpose lies within you. You detect it rather than invent it. It has made itself known in the activities and interests that have been important to you for years. A blueprint for your life's purpose has already been established and is your foundation. It's your individual design for a fulfilling life.

The blueprint has always been with you and tries to make itself known at different times in your life. You may experience this through your longings. Although not all longings should be followed, some cannot be denied. Being more mindful of your priorities and beliefs will help you clarify which longings to follow. You'll learn more in the next chapter.

What you focus on becomes your life. So if you focus on following your blueprint, it will become the guiding force in your life. If you get distracted with the mindless chatter within and around you, that also may become your life. Knowing what to overlook is an important aspect of attention management. And remember the mindful meditation exercises in the previous chapter. These are effective tools to improve your focus.

Figuring Out Your Blueprint

There are steps you can take to discern your blueprint. Direction is available as you travel the path so that the trail you leave behind when you die will be based on responsible decisions. Your trail is unique. For most of us, the trail contains some disappointment and regret. But it is hopeful to know that you can live a life that is more consistent with your priorities and beliefs.

Life has more meaning when you're striving for a purpose. With clients who want to discern their life's purpose, we start by asking a series of questions to explore what brought them joy and fulfillment as children. We ask how they expressed their creativity when they were young. We look for an underlying experience, the blueprint. Then we inquire to see if the essence of their experience is being expressed today. If memory is the most meaningful measure of attention (Langer 1997), then your memory of your early experiences shows what captured your attention as a child.

Let's see what shapes the blueprint of a friend of ours. Please be mindful as you complete these exercises about activities that you enjoyed as a child. Our friend gave us her list of what gave her joy:

When I was a child, I liked to:

Cuddle with my dog

Dress up in my mother's clothes

Pretend to marry my boyfriend

Play legal secretary with my sister

Go to school

Help my teacher

Ride my bike

Walk my dogs

Draw and write stories

Go fishing

What gave you enjoyment as a child? What activities made you feel good and gave you a sense of well-being? In your journal, write your list quickly and spontaneously. Don't censor or judge yourself— just let the list flow. Please don't worry if the list is too short or too long. There is no right or wrong here. It's your list; it's unique. The key is to write what comes to your mind about your experiences. Before you begin, breathe mindfully. Take three slow, deep breaths. Inspiration is as close as your breath. Now take out your journal and complete this sentence:

When I was a child, I liked to:

When you have generated a list of activities, pause. Now, beside each item on the list, note what quality the activity brought out in you. Was it play, adventure, a sense of belonging, nurturing others, being nurtured, mastery, feeling successful, being connected with nature, learning, teaching, or other qualities?

When our friend did this, her list of qualities looked like this:

Activity:	*Quality:*
Cuddle with my dog	Nurturing
Dress up in my mother's clothes	Belonging
Pretend to marry my boyfriend	Belonging
Play legal secretary with my sister	Listening and writing
Go to school	Studying and learning
Help my teacher	Helping others
Ride my bike	Exercising
Take my dogs on long walks	Exploring and adventure
Draw and write stories	Being creative
Go fishing	Being in nature and connecting spiritually

List your activities and the qualities brought out in you by each.

Now, on another page in your journal, repeat the list of qualities about your underlying experience that you just recorded. Then beside each quality, write what you're doing today that brings out that quality in you. How are the talents and interests you had as a child expressed in activities that bring you pleasure and fulfillment today?

This is the journal entry made by our friend:

Quality:	*How is it expressed today:*
Nurturing	Being with family, friends, and clients
Belonging	Being with family, friends; church activities

Listening and writing	Conducting therapy with clients
Studying and learning	Attending conferences and workshops, and reading
Helping others	Helping clients, friends, family, volunteering
Exercising	Walking and morning exercises
Exploring and adventure	Traveling
Being creative	Writing articles and books
Being in nature	Fishing and walking in the woods
Connecting spiritually	All of the above

After completing your list, write in your journal, in narrative form, about the blueprint you have just uncovered. Our friend wrote the following in her journal:

When I was a child, I liked to cuddle with my dog, dress up in my mother's clothes, and pretend to marry my boyfriend, Philip. I wanted to be married and have a family and dogs. As a child, I didn't have the words for it, but I needed a sense of belonging: belonging to myself, with others, and with a higher power so I could feel a connection with a greater whole. Today I feel that belonging when I'm with my friends, family, coworkers, clients, and my church group. I even feel it when I am alone. I am connected to a sense of something larger. A sense of belonging is an important part of my blueprint.

My dad was a lawyer, and when I was young, perhaps four or five years old, my sister and I took turns pretending to be a lawyer and legal secretary. I preferred the part of legal secretary because I liked taking dictation notes and doing research. It is very much like today. I'm a psychologist, not a legal secretary, but I find it fulfilling to listen to clients and take notes. I do research on what might help them and encourage clients as they begin to make changes in their lives. This is a deeply satisfying part of my life.

I also loved school as a child. I liked being a student; it was fun. As an adult, I enjoyed studying for my doctorate, attending conferences, and writing books and articles. The seeds of what is most enjoyable and meaningful in my life today were present from my early years

On vacation, I enjoyed deep-sea fishing. The fun for me was not in catching fish. Rather, I loved the rocking movement of the boat. And when I was in a boat in the ocean and couldn't see land, I saw a big blue circle around me. I felt very small. I sensed security and relief in my smallness. Of course, I didn't know this at the time, but as an adult I recognized that this was a type of spiritual experience for me. It gave me positive feelings and a sense of well-being.

Being near water is very important in my life. It is a source of peace for me. But I hadn't made the time for this in recent years, so my life was out of balance. I decided to remedy that. I learned to fly fish. I find it soothing to stand in the water and feel the river's current as it gently rocks my body. I watch the water to notice where the calm water meets the rapid stream. I cast to that seam because that's where the fish are. The rod and line are an extension of my body, so I don't need much strength, just balance and timing. I relax into the movement and cast my line. It reminds me of the ballet dancing I liked to do as a child. When backcasting, I must be patient and allow enough time for my line to unfurl. If I don't, my line gets tangled, and I cannot go forward with precision and grace. This is a lesson not just important in fly fishing, but in many areas of my life.

The seeds of passion for nurturing, belonging, teaching, helping others, adventure, creativity, being in nature, and connecting with spiritual experience existed from my childhood. When I engage in activities that express these qualities, my life feels full and meaningful.

You may be surprised with the results of this exercise. Many people find that their lives are out of balance with the qualities that were essential in childhood. They aren't expressing the qualities represented in their blueprints, and it affects their level of happiness and well being. Are there parts of your blueprint not being expressed today in your life?

Unhappiness often comes from the gap between what you are doing with your life and what you need to be doing. For example, if your talents and gifts are those of nurturing and teaching, are you engaged in activities that express those traits? You don't have to be employed as a teacher or professional caregiver. You can express your blueprint in caring for loved ones, volunteer work, and a number of other ways. Expressing most of the qualities in your blueprint can bring a stronger sense of purpose and meaning to your life. It is a start to remember what activities brought you joy as a child and define the underlying qualities (belonging, teaching, learning, being in nature, etc.). This provides you with your blueprint.

Now please use your journal and write what comes to mind when you consider the following questions. Before you begin, breathe mindfully. Take three slow, deep breaths. Inspiration is as close as your breath.

1. What is not being brought forth in your blueprint? What qualities are missing?

2. What activities do you need to focus on to find more fulfillment?

3. What challenges do you face?

4. How do you feel about those challenges?

5. Who do you need for help and support?

6. What would you be willing to give up to be more faithful to your blueprint?

BLUEPRINT EXAMPLES

Here are examples of completed Blueprint Exercises from some of our friends. (We changed their names.) As you review them, think about the variety of ways this activity can be done. There is really no right way to do it. It's most important to connect the core qualities from your childhood play with how those qualities are expressed in your life today. Use the narrative to reflect on the connection between your life activities today and the qualities you expressed as a child.

Roger		
When I was a child I enjoyed	**Quality**	**How the quality is expressed today**
Learning magic tricks to show my family and friends	Mastery and teaching	Working as a therapist—helping people solve problems in their lives
Riding my bike around the neighborhood with my friends	Connection with friends and adventure	Traveling with my wife and family; visiting with friends
Reading science fiction books and watching science fiction television programs and movies	Play and adventure	Still love to read science fiction; going to movies with my wife
Playing fantasy games like Dungeons and Dragons	Adventure, connection with others	Working as a therapist, helping clients slay their own dragons, of sorts
Creating and writing computer games	Learning and mastery	Writing, teaching
Drawing cartoons with my father	Learning, mastery, and connection	Drawing with and reading to my children
Building models	Play and mastery	Continual home-improvement projects

Journal Narrative About Blueprint

When I was young, I enjoyed learning about new things that I found interesting, like magic tricks, science, art, and model building. I loved to illustrate maps and descriptions of fantasy worlds I could lead my friends through in Dungeons and Dragons games. When not with friends, I could lose track of time (I now know this is called a "flow" experience) by sitting alone in my room, painting miniature figures and constructing castles and terrain to be used with friends when we would meet to play. I had forgotten until I am writing right now how much I enjoyed all aspects of these games. Doing this exercise, I am able to reignite my enthusiasm and feel again the excitement I had for this hobby as a child.

I also see now how my college and career path flows from these early passions. I began college as an art major at the University of the Arts in Philadelphia. I always enjoyed drawing and building things. What I really enjoyed creating was often more practical than artistic, however. I switched majors and colleges and completed my education in psychology and social work at the University of Pittsburgh and Marywood University. I was drawn toward my work as a therapist, social worker, and writer by the application of several of the qualities I enjoyed as a child. Some of these are: creative thinking, scientific theory, and my enjoyment of meeting with people to solve problems.

As a child I enjoyed building things and I still love to work on my house. I also love to play with my children, building things with building blocks, clay, snow, or whatever else we have.

I can see as I connect with my childhood passions, they are really the same things I enjoy doing in adulthood, only in forms that fit my life now. I still need to make room for escape and self-indulgent play, too. For this reason, a while ago I began reading science fiction novels each night in bed before I fall asleep. I actually only read for about ten to twenty minutes each night, but it allows me to connect to my love of fantasy, give a nod to my youth, and it spices up my dream life too!

Sue		
When I was a child I enjoyed	**Quality**	**How the quality is expressed today**
Reading	Learning new things and learning to enjoy quiet and being alone	Reading, valuing my solitude, taking trips by myself
Playing at being teenagers with my friends	Fantasizing, being creative, nurturing	Understanding my children, helping friends, doing work for my church, entertaining my children
Playing "executive and secretary" with friend	Organizing, leading, and being responsible	Running household, church work
Playing "traveling to Miami" with my friend	Organizing, fantasizing, and listening	Running my large household, being a nurse, doing church work, being a parent and a friend
Playing "mansion" with my friends	Organizing, fantasizing, belonging, and nurturing	Being with friends and family and working as a nurse
Riding my bike	Exercising, adventure, and exploring	Exercise 3x/week, hike and canoe in warm weather
Doing well in school	Studying, learning, writing, belonging	Reading, being part of a church community, connecting with my family and old friends
Writing stories	Writing and fantasizing	Letter writing, helping with others' manuscripts, and working on church projects
Having secrets with my brother	Belonging and listening	Being a parent and friend

Journal Narrative About Blueprint

My childhood activities definitely foreshadowed what my leanings were to be in adulthood. Many of my play activities centered around organizing people and information. One of my games with a friend featured us pretending to be mothers of eight or ten children each. We imagined ourselves living in a mansion. Our "husbands" were away most of the time, so we had primary responsibility for the children and household. We made elaborate charts to divide up the labor and to keep track of dental appointments, school conferences, who needed shoes, when the milkman was coming, what was for dinner, etc. Our mansion was a bustling, happy place that took some know-how to manage. We delighted in heaving sacks of breakfast cereal around, paring thirty pounds of potatoes at a sitting, and having the kids line up to get their hair combed in the morning—all imaginary, of course. The charts for remembering things were actually written out, though, and this brought me great satisfaction. I ended up having four children of my own and a husband whose work makes great demands on his time and energy. I have kept a list of things to do for the household and family members for twenty years now and would feel lost without that organizational tool.

I was a stutterer as a child, so I developed keen listening skills in order to compensate. I also lost myself in books and took to writing in order to communicate more smoothly. These pleasures and tools have carried over to the present. I find I can attain the state of "flow" when I'm reading or writing.

I was a responsible student, because I liked to organize my work and because that was a way of "belonging" as a stutterer. I was respected as a fine student even if I could not say my own name, for instance, or read aloud from a text in class. It was important to establish myself as an academic "player." I grew to love reading, writing, and listening. I am valued in my community even though I cannot always communicate reliably orally.

My nurturing outlets as a child—time with friends, writing my stories—were very satisfying. I went on to make that quality central in my adult life by becoming a nurse, by ascribing great importance to my role as a mother, and by keeping up longstanding friendships (some from childhood). These were and are my most fun times, most meaningful times, most rich times.

I am very happy with my little life in central Pennsylvania. There is more than enough here for me; I do not feel a need or desire to travel or have unusual adventures. Daily life and the surrounding two hundred miles are more than enough for me to deal with, to mine for riches, to keep up with, to appreciate in all its glory. Although I still like a nice bike ride, I don't seek foreign or risky experiences like I was doing with a bike ride around my neighborhood as a child. I remember a Mary Chapin-Carpenter song in which she sings about people who need adventure and living grander dreams. That is fine for them, but it's not for me.

Being alone is as important for me now as it was in my early years. I make time for it—I have always carved it out of whatever circumstances I have found myself in. I require quiet almost like food. I am fed spiritually if I get time to listen to my own thoughts and see where they take me.

In some ways, as I write this, I see that I am now just a physically larger and freer version of the little girl I was in the 1960s. I do what I need to do and love to do. I am lucky that at the same time I actually accomplish things, enhance other people's lives, and can lead a satisfying life of which I am proud.

Mary		
When I was a child I enjoyed	**Quality**	**How the quality is expressed today**
Singing	Entertaining	Telling stories to friends and children
Dancing	Physically connected to beauty	Practicing yoga
Reading	Imagining and escaping	Reading
Going to the movies	Imagining	Going to the movies
Daydreaming	Imagining	Daydreaming, doing guided imagery
Play acting	Entertaining	Public speaking
Arguing (and winning!)	Being right (Mastery)	Debating (win and lose)

Pretending to date Elvis Presley	Being special	I am married to a dark-haired man who loves music and thinks I'm special
Pretending to teach school	Helping others	Teaching others and counseling
Going to church	Spirituality, connection, and magic	Praying, meditating, and attending study groups

Journal Narrative About Blueprint

I was an only child for the first ten years of my life, so I had a vivid imagination. I also had a strong desire to belong and came to believe that if I were special, I would indeed belong in many places.

I was fascinated by the movies—all the stars seemed to live such glamorous lives. Growing up in the south, there was a high value placed on beauty, so I dreamed of singing, dancing, acting, and learning all manner of beauty secrets to feel as pretty as the stars. I would dance with my mother's old mop, drifting to a make-believe world where I wore beautiful evening gowns with flowing skirts.

I took dancing lessons as a young girl, mostly tap, ballet, and modern jazz, and when I danced, I was absolutely free, decidedly beautiful, and providing wonderful entertainment to the audience who attended the concerts in which I performed.

I also enjoyed debating, especially with my father. I like the process of critical, analytical thinking and often dreamed of becoming a trial lawyer.

Other people fascinated me—how they thought, what their lives were about—so psychology was a natural interest. Learning about human nature gave me a deep satisfaction, and discovering ways to be of support, comfort, and help to others gave a true richness to the meaning of my life.

I love the ocean, though I do not swim. It's the sound of the ocean that soothes me, comforts me, and that draws me near. When I meditate, I often play the sounds of the ocean in the background. I feel at peace.

The qualities that my early childhood experience brought to me remain the same qualities that I look for in my life today. In completing this exercise, I see many of the things that bring depth and purpose to my life. I also see things that I am missing or want more of—a good awareness for me.

Stan		
When I was a child I enjoyed	**Quality**	**How the quality is expressed today**
Going sled riding in the park	Excitement, fun, exhilaration	Not being expressed in my life today
Participating in arts and crafts at a local playground	Learning, being nurtured	Participating in a mentor program at work
Exploring and hiking in the woods and climbing rocks; building trails	Achievement, mastery, camaraderie, and leadership	Collaborating with coworkers on program design and implementation
Going on long-distance bike rides	Achievement, exploration, challenge, and companionship	Taking road trips and going on Sunday drives with my family
Being an altar boy	Accomplishment, conscientiousness, spirituality, and mastery	Being conscientious about my work performance
Playing games like kick-the-can on summer evenings	Connecting with nature, playfulness and fun	Going hiking and camping
Summertime picnics with my family	Being nurtured, sense of belonging and contentment	Meal time with my present family
Collecting pine cones for Christmas	Connecting with nature, being challenged, fun	Hiking and spending time in nature
Being sent to the candy store on visits to my grandparents	Adventure, being nurtured, fun	Visiting my in-laws, and visiting my own family back home
Going swimming	Fun, physical activity	Exercising regularly

Journal Narrative About Blueprint

I notice that several aspects of my childhood blueprint have been carried into my adulthood, while others have been somewhat neglected. I'm struck by the simplicity of my early pleasurable experiences. I enjoyed spending time outdoors. Hiking, swimming, playing kick-the-can, and going on long-distance bicycle rides underscore my love of nature, which continues to this day. I'm a family man now with a small child and don't go hiking and camping as often as I did when I was younger. Nonetheless, I always feel more relaxed when I take time to enjoy the outdoors.

I also notice that my recent marriage has strengthened several of the activities of youth that brought me happiness by providing a sense of belonging. For example, I think my life was somewhat out of kilter as a single man eating alone and not living with family. The happiness associated with family picnics or Sunday trips to my grandparents has been restored by having meals with my wife and daughter and by visiting relatives. This feeling of being nurtured and belonging to something greater than myself more than compensates for some of the adventurousness of childhood that had accompanied me into bachelorhood.

The childhood need to achieve that I noted in building trails in the woods or being able to serve Mass well as an altar boy are now expressed by my appreciation of challenges at work. I enjoy working with colleagues in designing and implementing programs, and I like my job to be somewhat challenging.

I think that the emphasis of the outdoors in my youth foreshadows a later interest in spirituality. This was evident, too, in my enjoyment in being an altar boy. As I've grown older, I've become increasingly comfortable with spiritual concerns, and I have come to place a lot of value on religious faith.

The part of my blueprint that startled me most was the absence of childhood playfulness and exhilaration that I knew with sled riding or racing across the lawn in the summer to kick the can. I think that my love of road trips and my connection to the outdoors is an attempt to rediscover some of this gleefulness. But I still need to play—especially now that I'm a husband and a father. Fortunately, I think that my one-year-old daughter and my wife are helping me to reclaim this part of my blueprint.

MEANINGFUL GOALS

In the beginning of this chapter, we talked about the pursuit of goals that give our lives meaning. You completed an exercise that specified what activities you liked as a child, what qualities were brought out in you by those activities and, finally, how the blueprint apparent in your childhood is being currently expressed. Then you wrote in your journal what you need in order to become more faithful to your blueprint today.

Now is a good time to make a commitment to yourself to increase your happiness and well-being by starting to incorporate some of the missing qualities into your life. If you can't imagine where you'll make the time to do this, there are some comments on simplifying your life in the next section that may help you. All by itself, your commitment to incorporate expression of some of these qualities is a start. Finding a balance is necessary so that you may build a solid footing. Then you can proceed to more adequately fulfill your life's purpose.

Recall that happiness is a byproduct of being engaged in activities and goals that give your life a sense of meaning and purpose. Review the exercises just completed, think about how the items in your blueprint fit into the following goals, and make some notes in your journal. Before you begin, breathe mindfully. Take three slow, deep breaths. Inspiration is as close as your breath.

1. Work and achievement: Are you committed to your work? Does it seem meaningful to you and others? Is it challenging to you?

2. Intimacy and relationships: How do you relate to others? Do you trust them? Are you helpful to others and let them know you care? Are you a good listener?

3. Religion and spirituality: Do you feel connected to something greater than yourself? How would you describe that connection? Are you part of a faith community?

4. Transcendence and generativity: Is it important to you to transcend your own interests and contribute to others, particularly younger people? Are you a good role model? Do you have concern and a commitment to future generations?

DO YOU FEEL PUSHED OR CALLED?

The word "fulfill" means "to perform a duty." It also means "to satisfy a desire." You can be pushed to perform duties and satisfy desires or you can be "called." There is a big difference between the experiences of being pushed and called to do something.

Being pushed may feel like you are being forced. There is often a sense of urgency. It seems natural to want to resist being pushed. You may feel stuck in dead-end ruts in areas of life that are no longer satisfying or engaging.

Being called, on the other hand, is to move to something because of attraction. Living a meaningful life feels like being called to satisfy your deepest desires. You may feel a strong attraction or longing for something holy, playful, and filled with an awareness of gratitude and love. Some describe being called as an experience of vivid engagement. It is when we are most fulfilled and most fully and gladly occupied. In the past, the word "calling" meant to be called by God to do good deeds. For some people, that is still the definition. For others, being called simply means contributing something of value to the world (Davidson and Caddell 1994). In this case, there may be no religious connection.

Your calling may be referred to as your vocation. You provide a service that is needed in the world. It is "the place where your deep gladness and the world's deep hunger meets" (Buechner 1993, 119). It is a challenge to be who you were born to be—a combination of your natural talents, interests, and acquired skills. The blueprint for your vocation and calling was evident in your childhood activities. That is why we asked you to be mindful in your completion of the exercises in this chapter. Parker Palmer (2000) writes about a Hasidic tale told by Martin Buber (1955). Rabbi Zusya believed that in the coming world he would not be asked "Why were you not Moses." Rather the question would be "Why were you not Zusya?"

In your journal, record your thoughts about the difference between being pushed and called. When do you feel pushed? When do you feel called? Give examples. This could take some time to think through, so know that you can take your time. If you don't want to do this exercise now, you can come back to it later.

A retired friend of ours considered these questions of being pushed versus being called and wrote the following in his journal:

I feel pushed when there are a lot of things that need to be done for the church and our home at the same time. For example, I need to prepare something for the church finance committee and the wood needs splitting and hauling in before it snows. I enjoy splitting wood, and I enjoy working with the numbers for the finance committee. It's not the tasks themselves that dictate whether I feel pushed. It is having to do too many things at the same time that makes me feel that way.

I feel called when I do something that helps someone. When I was volunteering at the elementary school a few years ago, I really felt called. Now I feel called when I can make something for someone else. I am thinking of the tool boxes I made for our three children last Christmas and a cuttingboard holder I made for Mary this past week. Or when I prepare a report that's well put together and helps our church, or when I can clean up the horses and the barn. Other examples include installing the stone edging around the back of the house and power-washing and staining the barn. I feel called when I am a greeter at church, meeting new people and helping them feel welcome.

Guided Meditation

This simple meditation may further clarify the difference between being called and pushed. You may want to tape record this meditation or have someone read it to you. The meditation should be read slowly. Pause for about five seconds where there is a break in the text. Close you eyes, relax, take a few deep, mindful breaths, and listen to the words

Focus on your breathing . . . In and out . . . No need to change it—just be aware of it . . . Hear the sounds around you . . . Feel the temperature of the room . . .

Imagine leaving the building you're in and comfortably walking along a river . . . Come to an area of trees with a path leading into it. Follow the path into the woods . . . Pay attention to the sights and sounds . . . Take your time . . .

---

*Enter a grove of old trees. The earth is soft beneath your feet
... At a small clearing, there is an ancient door in the side of
the mountain. See it in your mind ... Place your hand on the
handle. The door opens easily ... Stand in a large, beautiful
cavern ... You are surprised to see pictures of yourself along
the wall. There are two sections of pictures. One set of pictures
shows you when you are being pushed. Look at them now ...*

---

*The other set shows you when you're being called forth, doing
what is natural and experiencing pleasure. Now look at these
pictures ...*

Notice what you're feeling ... Take your time.

---

*When you're finished, turn and walk to the door ... It opens
easily. Notice that you are back on the path in the wooded area
... Now you see the path along the river, and you return to
the building ... Return to this room, to the present time ...
Slowly and gently return to awareness of your breathing and
open your eyes.*

Begin writing about your experience in meditation. Please take
time to record your insights in your journal. You will refer to them later
to build your motivation to stay on your path. Before you begin,
breathe mindfully. Take three slow, deep breaths. Inspiration is as close
as your breath.

In what pictures did you see yourself being pushed? How did it
feel? In what pictures did you see your being called? How did it feel?

A friend of ours wrote in his journal:

*In my meditation, there was only one picture of me being
pushed. It was higher than the others, and it showed me with
a frantic look on my face. My hands were up, next to my head,
and there was a look of "stop" on my face. I wanted to say
"go away and stop bothering me." I felt like there was just not
enough time. I was feeling very revved up.*

On the other wall was a picture of me with a group of school kids. We were all standing together as if posing for a picture. We were all smiling and happy, glad to be with each other. The feelings I saw in those pictures were contentment, calmness, and serenity. I was happy.

A meditation like this one can help you remember when you felt pushed or called. It probably comes as no surprise to you that some of the activities you discovered in your meditation corresponded to the valued qualities in your list of childhood activities. It makes sense that there would be connections. This is where your blueprint lies. Go back to review the list of goals earlier in this chapter. Do you have anything new to add to the list? If so, please do that now.

Many of us work for a living. Do you feel pushed or called at work? It's not surprising that people who feel called find that work is more fulfilling and rewarding (Wrzesniewski, et al. 2002). They tend to spend more time at work (even if they are not paid to do so) and they may even enjoy their work more than leisure time. People who don't feel called in their work tend to find other activities more rewarding.

There are three ways that people view their experience of work (Schwartz 1986). Some see work as a job for the purpose of financial support so that they may enjoy other interests that bring them greater satisfaction. Others see work as a career and appreciate the status, prestige, and increased income that come with advancement. Finally, there are people who see their work as a calling. They do not work primarily for advancement of their careers or financial reward. Rather, they work for the sense of fulfillment they get from the work itself because, even if only in a small way, they believe they are contributing to make the world a better place. Of course, people may experience their work as a combination of these categories.

If you're employed, how do you experience your work? Is it a job, a career, a calling, or a combination of these? Are you able to respond to your calling because you support yourself with a job? If you are not employed and spend your time doing something else, do you see yourself as preparing for a job or a career? Are you currently living in a way consistent with your calling? (For example, some people stay at home for the purpose of caring for children or others.) Write about your experience of work in your journal and pay attention to how this fits into the activities in your blueprint.

YOUR INTELLIGENCE

Your blueprint probably contains evidence of multiple types of intelligence. There are at least eight distinct forms of intelligence, according to Dr. Howard Gardner, a professor of education at Harvard University (Gardner 1997). We are all familiar with the intelligences of language and logic since these are valued in IQ testing and school performance. But there are other intelligences, too. There is a musical intelligence related to perceiving and creating music. Spatial intelligence gives us the capacity to appreciate space and spatial relationships. Our bodily kinesthetic intelligence permits us to use our bodies in various ways. Botanists, skilled hunters, and fishermen/women share an intelligence about the natural world. Finally, there are two forms of intelligence that relate to understanding people. One form relates to understanding others and one form relates to understanding ourselves. We all have some degree of these intelligences. Obviously, we are unique in how we manifest their combination. This may be a good time to review your blueprint and write about which intelligences are involved in the activities.

A friend made this entry in his journal:

The activities of making things, whether small or large wood projects or major home improvements, probably requires spatial intelligence, although they aren't all that complex. What I use more is my ability to understand others. Most of my professional career was in medicine, where making the diagnosis is only a part of the task. The bigger part, in my mind, was recognizing where the parents were in their relations with their child and helping them in that area. Now retired, I enjoy being with people. When people tell me that I am "good" with people, it always surprises me since I remember, as a young adult, how nervous I usually was when I had to interact with someone new.

VITAL ENGAGEMENT AND THE FLOW STATE

Some people go through life without a sense of purpose. They subscribe to the motto "Life's a bitch, and then you die." Other people, with similar actual circumstances, savor life and become deeply involved in activities. They have a sense of purpose and meaning. Finding enjoyment and meaning in life has been called *vital engagement* (Nakamura 1995). Vital engagement has two stages: enjoyable participation and meaningful interaction (Nakamura and Csikszentmihalyi 2002). The key to vital engagement is to selectively focus our attention, participate in activities that bring meaning to our lives, and form goals to keep the process going. Research has shown that continued active participation is associated with physical and emotional well-being for people as they age (Rowe and Kahn 1998). This comes as no surprise.

Some activities are rewarding in and of themselves. They have intrinsic value, invisible to the eye. We don't need an external reward for performing these tasks. The process itself is reinforcing. Intrinsic value and fulfillment are closely related (Wrzesniewski et al. 2002). You may have a number of these activities in your blueprint. Total involvement in the moment has been called the *flow state* (Csikszentmihalyi 1990). When you are in the flow state you are mindfully engaged and lose self-consciousness. You feel challenged and have a sense that you can handle whatever comes next. Time has an elastic quality. It may slow down or accelerate. Finally, regardless of the outcome, the process has totally compelled your attention.

Be mindful as you review your blueprint. You may notice that some of your activities could be characterized as vital engagement and flow state. Put a star beside each of these activities. Do you have a goal to increase opportunity for these experiences? Write your thoughts and feelings in your journal. It may help to build your motivation to clear a space in your life for what matters to you. Speaking of clearing a space, this is what a friend wrote in her journal:

> *When I wanted to make several big changes in my life, I knew I had to clear some space in my calendar so I could meditate, write in my journal, and spend time in nature to mindfully increase my focus on what mattered to me.*
>
> *I used a memory device to help me remember not to take on new commitments and to reduce some of the commitments I had already scheduled. This device was a necklace. I wore it every day as a reminder. It was a thin chain with a small, delicate disc hanging from it. The disc had a hole in the middle of it. Many times each day, I reached for my necklace and felt the empty space in the middle of the disc. This reminded me to*

*clear a space in order to pay attention to what really mattered
to me. I wanted clarity. I had to simplify so that I could focus
on the present moment with compassion, purity, and full
attention.*

Now make a few notes in your journal as you consider these
questions:

1. Is there a memory device you can use to remind yourself
   daily to focus on clearing a space for what matters in your
   life?

2. List ideas for other ways to remind yourself to simplify your
   life.

3. What will you do less of as you begin to clear more space?

A friend made this entry in his journal:

*I have used a calendar, and that seems the most effective.
Or I use three-by-five cards and write on them what I want
to do (but am likely to neglect). Then I keep the card in view.
If I needed to clear a space for some activity. I would cut down
on the time I spent on a less-important task. For example, I'd
probably clean the barn in less time and tell myself that the job
was good enough.*

NOTES ON SIMPLIFICATION

For many years, advocates of simple living have challenged materialism
and consumerism. Historians tell us that during the Revolutionary
War, the Civil War, and the First and Second World Wars, the
emphasis was on living a simple and focused life. However, after those
wars ended, Americans went on major spending sprees, and our deeper
insights diminished in the presence of the increase in spending and
consumption (Segal 1999). On a daily basis, our world becomes
increasingly more complex. Clearly, it's time to simplify.

Many self-help books teach us how to simplify our lives. Much of
the literature states that we have more money and more stuff than we
need. Certainly, most of us can cut down a little on spending, but only
10 to 15 percent of Americans have much more money and resources

than they need (Segal 1999). The other 85 to 90 percent of us have to struggle to produce enough income so our families can have adequate food, housing, health care, education, and retirement. We have seen a significant increase in the income needed to provide for these core needs.

Jerome M. Segal, Senior Research Scholar at the University of Maryland Institute for Philosophy and Public Policy, believes that after 9/11/01 our focus on living simply was dwarfed by threats of terrorism and our response to those threats. In his book, *Graceful Simplicity*, Segal argues that, as Americans, we do not use our resources efficiently and until we make systematic changes, we will not be able to transition into shorter work weeks, affordable day care, or adequate housing, healthcare, and retirement (1999). It is far beyond the scope of this book to tackle this topic of simple living in detail, but we recommend reading Segal's book if you are interested in pursuing this further.

We recognize that happiness doesn't come from pursuing higher income and greater consumption. Life is not just about making and having money, but it is important to have adequate material resources to cultivate what Aristotle called "goods of the soul," which are courage and wisdom (Segal 1999). If we don't focus on the nonmaterial as we become absorbed with our careers and monetary growth, we end up feeling empty. If we have a moderate supply of money and resources, we can keep our personalities intact by staying focused on what matters to us in nonmaterial ways. More is not better when it comes to focusing on acquisition and consumption.

Making Time

It takes time to make time. Can you free up fifteen to thirty minutes a day to consider what really matters? Remember, the best way to avoid change is to maintain a complicated life. On your deathbed, you won't say: "I wish I had spent more time at work and bought more stuff." You'll probably wish you had spent more time with loved ones or made a greater contribution to someone or something important to you.

Take a minute to think about what you would say if you were on your deathbed. What would you wish you had done more of in your life? Write about this in your journal. Before you begin, breathe mindfully. Take three slow, deep breaths. Inspiration is as close as your breath.

Good parents use careful attention and loving discipline to nurture their child's development. Like a good parent, you will need to pay attention and be disciplined in how you spend your time, since your focus becomes your life.

You are reading this book, so you must want to increase meaningful activity, consistent with your sense of purpose in life. You may need to simplify so that you can focus with compassion, purity, and full attention on what really matters to you.

Simplifying your life does not take much time or money. Guidelines are available to help you reduce clutter, organize your possessions, streamline your work habits, eliminate nonessential activity, and find more time for meaningful pursuits. Several books listed in the references could be helpful to you.

One of the common suggestions about how to simplify is to reduce clutter. For example, if you have piles of paper, articles, and magazines, you may want to get rid of them. These piles represent a lack of decision making. They take space and energy because each time your gaze flits over them, a small voice in your head says, "I need to do something with those." Yet, most of us leave the pile sitting there. You may delay starting to work on the project because the job seems overwhelming. The best way to begin removing the clutter is to set a timer for fifteen minutes and work on the piles for that amount of time. When the timer goes off, stop work and walk away. Organize everything into three piles: important, urgent, and interesting. Do not add new stuff to the piles. The important thing is to work no longer than fifteen minutes at a time. Gradually the piles will begin to shrink. You will be delighted and probably amazed at how easy this is. If piles are a problem for you, you may find this strategy effective.

Elaine St. James has written best-selling books about simplifying your life. Here are a few of her suggestions:

1. Resign from any groups where you dread spending time.

2. Work where you live or close to it.

3. Watch less TV and cancel half your magazine subscriptions.

4. At least once a week, be in bed by 9 P.M.

5. Keep asking, "Is this going to simplify my life?"

6. Less is more: Reduce the clutter in your house and office.

7. Just say no to new obligations and stuff you don't really need.

In your journal, list two things you will do within the next week to free up some time and energy. Where will you focus the time and energy that will become available to you? Review the list of goals you made earlier in this chapter and note in your journal where your "new" time and energy can be focused. Before you begin, breathe mindfully. Take three slow, deep breaths. Inspiration is as close as your breath.

If you need motivation for following through with simplification, review your blueprint of talents, interests, and strengths from your journal. This will reinforce that you want to spend more time engaged in activities filled with meaning and purpose. You will need to spend less of your time with activities that aren't that important. It may be helpful to tell a close friend about your plans to simplify and ask for support.

- In your journal, write about what you want to spend more time doing.

- Who can you talk to for support in simplifying your life?

- When will you call this person and discuss this?

Simplifying your surroundings can help you simplify your life and free-up time. Make a commitment to yourself now. If you are stuck and unable to simplify your life to spend more time in meaningful activity, please read a book on this topic (listed in the reference section) or talk with a coach or therapist. You do have the ability to engage in activities that bring more meaning and purpose to your life. There is no time like the present to commit to doing this and to begin to take steps in this direction. Life is precious, and time is limited. We have today. Someday it will be otherwise.

Chapter 4

Spirituality

We have religion when we have an abiding gratitude for all that we have received. We have religion when we look upon people with all their failings and still find them good, when we look beyond people to the grandeur in nature and to the purpose in our own heart. We have religion when we have done all we can, and then in confidence entrust ourselves to the life that is larger than ourselves.

—Excerpt from "Impassioned Clay"
by Ralph N. Halverson*

In the last chapter you examined what activities and goals are fulfilling to you. You began to make decisions about how to simplify your life

---

* Reprinted by permission of the Unitarian Universalist Association

and filter out distractions. Using your blueprint, you developed goals, for what matters in your life. However, you would probably agree that to have a life worth living, we can't just do what feels good and seems right. We do need some guidelines to follow. Connecting talents and interests to spiritual practices, beliefs, and experiences helps us to further clarify what is meaningful and worthy of our focus. This chapter will help with those connections.

First, we'll look broadly at the topics of spirituality and religion. Then we will focus on the practices, beliefs, and experiences of spirituality. As we do this, we'll take a look at the research concerning the benefits of spiritual and religious practices on physical and emotional health. You will write a spiritual autobiography to clarify how your meaningful activity connects with your spiritual journey. This chapter is written from a psychological and research perspective. There is no attempt to convince you to adopt any practice or belief that is not consistent with your spiritual, religious, or secular orientation. Please note that for the sake of inclusion, we will use the term "higher power" to mean God or any other experience of connection to something greater than oneself. Our goal is simply to help you clarify what you believe and see how it relates to the meaningful activities in your daily life.

SPIRITUALITY AND RELIGION

Spirituality and religion are sometimes used interchangeably. They share an appreciation of the sacred that is coupled with having an experience of connection beyond the self—often referred to as transcendence. While there are characteristics in common between spirituality and religion, it is helpful to draw some distinctions.

Religion is an organized social institution with specific beliefs about the nature of God or a higher power. In religion there are specific beliefs about how the individual should relate to that higher power. Most Americans who say they are religious report that they are Christians or Jews. However, there are a growing number of members of immigrant communities who describe themselves as Hindu, Muslim, Buddhist, or members of other non-Judeo-Christian religions (Peterson and Seligman 2004).

The word spirituality comes from the Latin *spiritis,* and it means breath. Your connection with spirituality is as close as your breath. You had practice with this connection in chapter 2, with the mindfulness meditations. Unlike religion, spirituality is more an attribute of the specific person, like character or personality (Miller and Thoreson 1999). Spirituality is usually described as a personal quest for understanding the meaning of life and understanding a relationship with a higher power. The quest may involve a community with religious rituals. But even in community, spirituality is a private experience from which energy, inspiration, and meaning are received. Spiritual experiences are not prescribed by any doctrine. Rather, they are individual and range from contemplation in nature to feeling sacred in connection with others. A person's spirituality may include a religion, but not necessarily.

Spirituality and religion may be different in concept, since spirituality is a characteristic of the individual and religion is a set of rules or beliefs held by a group of people. However, sometimes they are hard to tell apart, as they are in the opening reading from Halverson.

Spirituality and religion have three domains: practice, belief, and experience (Miller and Thoreson 1999). Spiritual and religious practices can include contemplation, prayer, meditation, reading faith literature, rituals, fasting, and contributing to others' lives. Religious practices may also include worship services, public prayer, singing, and study of scripture. The second domain of spirituality and religion includes beliefs about the transcendent and about personal values and morals. The third domain is that of experience. This area is more of a challenge to define. Believers and non-believers have similar experiences, but the meaning they attribute to those experiences differs widely. For example, a believer may attribute a spiritual explanation to a particular experience, and a nonbeliever may attribute the same experience to coincidence or chance.

PRACTICES

We will now examine what we know about the benefits of engaging in some important spiritual practices. We include prayer, meditation, participation in religious services, participation in a religious community, and community service.

Prayer

Michael E. McCullough and David R. Larson have reviewed research about who prays and under what circumstances (1999). We think you will find their results and conclusions interesting, so we share them here. In the United States, most people pray and they believe their prayers are heard and answered at times. People pray to cope with problems and to deal with fear and loss. Most people who pray would rather pray silently and alone rather than aloud in groups. Older people pray more often than the young. People who are more empathic and thoughtful pray more often than those who lack empathy and a conscience. Mothers in low-violence neighborhoods pray less than mothers in high-violence areas. People with more severe problems pray more frequently than people with less severe problems. Among recovering alcoholics, the frequency of prayer is associated with having a sense of purpose in life. People who pray frequently appear to be more likely to avoid high levels of stress. In addition, after serious life stressors, people who pray frequently are less likely to have physical and emotional problems. While these results are interesting, remember that the apparent advantages of frequent prayer may also be explained by the use of other religious, spiritual, or secular coping strategies, such as seeking the support of others. In addition, there have been negative health effects found when the people who pray believe that God is punishing them and feel discontented with their relationship with a higher power or their religious support system.

Do you pray for guidance? Do you pray for others? Do you pray to grow closer in your connection with a higher power? Do you not pray at all? Throughout the years, scholars have attempted to identify the various types of prayer. For our purposes, we will use the five categories of prayer developed by the scholars Paloma and Pendleton (1989) and modified by McCullough and Larson (1998). While there are no universally accepted definitions of these forms of prayer, there are certain characteristics that define each category. As you read, think about how and under what circumstances you have used these forms of prayer, and make a few notes in your journal for later reference.

CONTEMPLATIVE AND MEDITATIVE PRAYER

Contemplative and meditative prayer involves a sense of intimacy in the personal connection with a higher power. This form is sometimes connected with growth after a stressful event. This may be prayer without specific direction. In the Christian tradition, this involves listening for messages from a higher power. In Judaism, there is a tradition of silent prayer. In the eastern tradition, meditation involves a clearing of the mind for the purpose of increased clarity and focus. Contemplative-meditative prayer can be associated with a sense of well-being and a reduction of psychological problems such as anxiety and anger. The mindfulness meditations in the previous chapter could be included in this category of prayer. Have you used contemplative-meditative prayer after a stressful event in your life? Do you recall the effects of using that prayer? It might be helpful for future exercises if you write about that experience in your journal.

RITUAL PRAYER

When you repeat a specific prayer from written material or memory, this is called *ritual prayer*. The evidence for the benefits of ritual prayer is not clear. Ritual prayer may be less associated with a sense of well-being, and people who rely on this form of prayer may have higher levels of negative feelings. Has ritual prayer been the only or primary form of prayer you have used? What has been the effect? Write about that in your journal.

PETITIONARY PRAYER

When you ask a higher power to grant a specific request, it's called *petitionary prayer*. Historically, this is one of the oldest forms of prayer. People who use only petitionary forms of prayer are often characterized as being in significant distress. On the other hand, if petitionary prayer is not the only form of prayer used, it is then more associated with religious and spiritual well-being. Have you used petitionary prayers? What were the circumstances? How have these prayers affected you? Write about this in your journal.

COLLOQUIAL PRAYER

Prayers that are conversations with a higher power are referred to as *colloquial prayers*. Although there may be petitionary requests, these prayers are more general in asking for strength, guidance, and wisdom as opposed to specific outcomes. These prayers can increase a feeling of intimacy with a higher power and the content ranges from problem solving to asking for blessings for others. People who frequently use colloquial prayer appear to have greater life satisfaction and a sense of well-being. Do you have conversations with a higher power? Can you recall specific times that you received clarity and strength from these conversations? Please make a few notes about this in your journal.

INTERCESSORY PRAYER

Praying for others is called *intercessory prayer* and is common in many religious traditions, including but not limited to Christianity, Judaism, and Islam. Studies of this type of prayer go back to 1872 (McCullough and Larson 1999). Larry Dossey (1993) and other researchers maintain that intercessory prayers bring benefit to those who are prayed for, even if those prayed for don't know prayers are being made for them. While there is some debate about how much benefit the subject of these prayers receives, one thing appears clear: the person who prays for others receives the benefit of increased well-being. Have you prayed for others? What has been the result? Write about this in your journal.

OTHER PRAYERS

You may be familiar with two other categories of prayer. Prayers of adoration offer praise and thanks for blessings. In confessional prayer, you confess wrongdoings and ask a higher power for forgiveness. Write in your journal about whether you have used these prayers and, if so, what has been the result? Think about significant times in your life when prayer has or hasn't helped. What was the impact on you?

Meditation

Meditation can be used as a secular relaxation strategy. It can also be used to develop mindfulness at a physical, emotional, and spiritual level. All spiritual and religious traditions have some form of meditation. There are basically two forms: mindfulness meditation and concentration meditation (Marlatt and Kristeller 1999). Mindfulness meditation is used primarily for deepening insight. In mindfulness meditation we become aware of our experience in the present moment. This awareness is coupled with an attitude of acceptance and lack of judgment as the observing self simply recognizes that thoughts are just thoughts and feelings are just feelings, and neither are mandates for action. Ironically, stepping outside of the self allows us insight that is not possible otherwise. With this insight, we become less reactive and have more choices about how to participate in the world.

Concentration meditation, on the other hand, allows the meditator to pay attention to something specific, like the awareness of breathing. Other forms of concentration meditation involve focusing on a visual object like a candle or mandala, or concentration on a word or a sound. Of course, these two types of meditation are often combined. For example, the meditator may begin by focusing awareness on her breath or some other object of concentration then move to awareness and insight about experience in the present moment. Both concentration and mindfulness meditation permit recognition of the constantly changing nature of reality.

Marlatt and Kristeller suggest that there are several effects of meditation procedures (1999). Meditation can have the effect of being very relaxing and can provide a pathway to change neurological processing. When we meditate, we enter a different physiological state in that we use less oxygen and relax our muscles and nervous system. Our brain wave activity also changes. Not surprisingly, meditation has been successfully incorporated into treatments for anxiety. Meditation can be considered a positive addiction because the effects are rewarding in and of themselves. The effects are similar to other healthy lifestyle habits, including exercise. Glasser states that to be a positive addiction, an activity must be easily accomplished, have positive value, be noncompetitive, and be done without self-criticism (1976). Meditation meets all of Glasser's criteria. But like everything else, meditation can be overdone. For example, too much meditation or exercise can direct attention away from relationships and goals in other areas.

Finally, meditation can be used as a spiritual practice. It is an effective way to increase an inner calm and feeling of serenity. Meditators often report an experience of transcendence, which is important in spiritual practice. Meditation also allows us to focus away from trivial annoyances and daily distractions.

You've already learned about mindfulness meditation in some detail; we won't repeat that here. However, before we leave this topic, please take a few moments to consider if your experience of meditation is different from your experience of prayer. Do you combine prayer and meditation in your spiritual practice? Write in your journal about your insights and experiences of prayer and meditation.

Religious Services and Spiritual Community

Participation in religious services and being part of a spiritual community have benefits for physical and emotional health. Most of the research refers to religious involvement, so it is not separated from spiritual practice. However, taken as a whole, this research points to numerous advantages of being involved in religious communities (Koenig et al. 2001). Religious participation is associated with a variety of health benefits: less coronary artery disease, fewer strokes, less hypertension, immune-system strengthening, less incidence of cancer, and fewer negative health behaviors (smoking, drug and alcohol addiction, high-risk sexual behaviors, etc.). What about the effects of religious involvement on mental health? Clearly, the research shows that religion has positive effects in a variety of areas: increased levels of self-esteem, well-being, happiness, life satisfaction, hope, optimism, purpose, and meaning in life. Religion is also associated with greater social support, offering less loneliness, better adaptation to grief, lower depression and suicide rates, less psychosis, reduced drug and alcohol use, less delinquency and criminal activity, and greater marital stability and satisfaction. Let's look more closely at some of the research.

Generally, in Judeo-Christian populations, greater self-esteem is associated with more religious involvement. Feelings of self-worth tend to be lower when there is little religious commitment. This may be due to the fact that some teachings discourage both excessive pride and self-condemnation while promoting a healthier view of self (Koenig 1994). Indicators of well-being (greater happiness, life satisfaction, positive morale, and good feelings) are consistently linked to religious practices and beliefs. This was the finding of 80 percent of the 100 studies that looked at this relationship (Koenig et al. 2001). In addition, 80 percent of the studies reviewed showed a positive correlation between religious involvement and greater hope and optimism about the future. Where there is a belief in the miraculous, there is always hope (Koenig et al. 2001).

The majority of studies demonstrate that religious people have a sense of purpose and meaning. In some religions, this relates to the sense that each person plays an important role in what is seen as the Divine Plan (Koenig et al. 2001). All world religions encourage the help and support of others (Coward 1986). So it makes sense that there is a connection between religious involvement and greater social support, both giving and receiving. Studies have found that church members provide the majority of support for older Americans with no family (Koenig, Moberg and Kvale 1988).

People who attend religious services are significantly less lonely and depressed than those who don't (Koenig et al. 2001). Not only are religiously active people less likely to be depressed, but when they do get depressed, they feel low for shorter periods of time than people without religious involvement. As you might expect, religious involvement tends to lower the rate of suicidal thoughts and suicidal attempts (Grunebaum et al. 2004). A lower suicide rate is found for Jews, Catholics, Baptists, Mormons, and Protestants. However, the research shows that Protestants are more likely than other religious groups to attempt suicide (Koenig et al. 2001).

Significantly less fear and anxiety is reported among the more religious. Less schizophrenia and fewer other psychoses are reported for these groups as well (Koenig et al. 2001). Religious people appear less likely to take illicit drugs and abuse alcohol. This is especially true for younger people. Less frequent drug and alcohol use in adolescence is associated with better health and greater success for people throughout their lives (Koenig et al. 2001). In a study of 11,995 high school seniors, researchers found that those who regularly attended church services were less likely to get into legal trouble. This was true everywhere in the United States except for the Pacific Northwest (Stark 1996).

Ninety percent of the studies reviewed in a large compilation of research showed that greater marital happiness, lower separation and divorce rates, and greater family stability is found among the religious (Koenig et al. 2001). This also affects the physical and mental health of the parents and children, since separation and divorce are associated with higher rates of problems in these areas. However, research also shows that men who have more conservative religious views than their wives are at increased risk to perpetrate domestic violence (Ellison et al. 1996). We will say more about the negative effects of religion below.

Clearly, religious participation and spiritual practices have many benefits—from a greater ability to relax to improved physical and mental health. The most significant motivation to explore religion and spirituality initially may be to free yourself from suffering. To pray and meditate only when you are upset, angry, jealous, or unhappy is a start, but re-establishing equilibrium isn't the only reason for spiritual practice. You can also develop better, kinder relationships and become more compassionate in the world.

Are women more religious than men? While they may appear to attend worship services more frequently, the answer is more complex (Peterson and Seligman 2004). It is not sex that makes the difference. Rather it is a person's gender orientation. Generally men and women who tend to be nurturing, gentle, conforming, and submissive tend to be more religious in this country. However, Jewish and Muslim men appear to be more religious than women in those faiths since they pray more frequently and study religious texts more often than women. So, the gender pattern is not universal but is influenced by culture as well.

The research also shows that there are times when religion can have a negative influence. For example, excessive devotion to religious practices can lead to the neglect of family and loved ones. Rigid interpretation of scripture can lead to mental or physical abuse of children or spouses. Rigidity can also foster excessive guilt over real or imagined sins and create harsh, judgmental, or aggressive attitudes. Overreliance on religion can keep people from seeking help that is needed to adequately treat physical and emotional problems. Negative religious coping (like believing God is punishing them or believing that illness is the work of the Devil) contributes to increased distress, depression, and anxiety (Ano and Vasconcelles 2005). Finally, consider how many lives have been lost in wars fought for religious reasons.

There are some people who don't want to pursue spirituality or religion (Pargament 1997). Perhaps they have felt bereft in loss or pain and were not comforted by a religious underpinning. In some cases, they have not been able to reconcile the concept of evil or adversity being allowed by a loving God. Finally, some people find religion incompatible with reason, logic, and science.

Community Service

Contributing time, talent, and other resources is a practice in many spiritual and religious traditions. Research has provided an analysis of how contributing to others benefits the helper (Midlarsky 1991). By contributing, the helper is distracted from his or her own difficulties. Giving to others can increase positive mood and enhance the sense of meaning in life for the helper while increasing his or her social skills and interpersonal relationships. These "volunteer effects" are greater for the elderly and the more religious. When people feel obligated to help others, rather than giving freely of their time, the helpers experience less positive effects (Piliavin 2003).

How do you contribute to the lives of others? You can volunteer with a church, school, service organization, or social agency. You can practice small acts of kindness on your own. Have you developed more compassion for other people as a result of contributing? Was your compassion based on religious, spiritual, or secular views? Think about these questions and write in your journal about your contributions to others and how the act of helping has affected you. Write about the benefits you have experienced as a result of sharing your time, talent, and resources with others.

BELIEFS

Our beliefs can affect us deeply on a physical, emotional, and spiritual level. There was an interesting study done in 1993 (Phillips, Ruth, and Wagner) about Chinese Americans and their beliefs. In Chinese culture, there are two basic beliefs that focus on astrology. One belief is that a person's life is strongly affected by the astrological year of the person's birth. The second belief is that body organs and illnesses are connected to astrological years. So the year of a person's birth is connected to the illness that the person is likely to die from. When a Chinese American who is a strong believer in this connection gets an illness predicted by his or her birth year, that person is more likely to die up to five years earlier than would be expected. The more strongly a person is attached to this belief, the more likely it is that he or she will die earlier than someone with the same illness born in a different year. Believers think they have little or no control over their fate, and their lives are shortened accordingly (Ray 2004).

Along similar lines is the study of the number of deaths the week before and the week after the Chinese Harvest Moon Festival (Phillips and Smith 1990). Elderly Chinese women view this holiday as having special significance since they become the center of activity and attention on this day. For Chinese women age seventy-five and older, the mortality rate decreases by 33 percent the week before the Harvest Moon Festival and increases by 35 percent the week after. Younger women have no such decrease or increase during this period (Ray 2004). For Jewish men, there is a similar decrease in mortality rates before Passover and a similar increase in mortality rates afterward. However, in both the case of the elderly Chinese women and the Jewish men, the connection between the holiday and mortality only applies to three classes of natural deaths: deaths due to strokes, heart attacks, and cancer. These are the three leading causes of deaths in this country, responsible for 60 percent of all deaths (Ray 2004). The death rates caused by infection and other problems were not similarly affected.

Andrew Newberg, from the University of Pennsylvania, has been studying the religious experiences of Buddhist monks and Franciscan nuns (2001). His research tells us something about religious experience and belief systems. Through brain scans, Newberg identified the area of the brain that is important in religious and spiritual experience. This area is also involved with the subjective sensation of time and space between the self and others. Both nuns, when praying, and monks, when meditating, had the same experience in their brains but they interpreted the experience differently. The nuns reported a feeling of closeness to Jesus while the Buddhist monks reported a feeling of connection with everything and everyone.

While Newberg researches brain activity, Dean Humer explores the genetic component of religious and spiritual experience (2004). Humer makes the controversial argument that spirituality is a universal experience that is hardwired in the brain through our genetic code. He measured people's ability to experience connection to a larger whole, feeling at one with something other than themselves.

Then he looked at twins and found a strong genetic connection in their capacity to experience connection to a larger whole. He discovered that this genetic relationship appears stronger than environmental factors such as religious education. Humer believes he isolated the "God gene" (VMAT2). He asserts that this gene affects the brain chemistry (monoamines) that appears to affect spiritual experience. He further argues that this gene and resulting chemistry may program some people with a predisposition to effectively overcome adversity. These assumptions are speculative at this point, but interesting research is continuing regarding the effect of biology on spiritual experience and belief.

Twelve-Step Program Beliefs

Before we look at core belief systems of religion and spirituality, we want to briefly review the beliefs of 12-step programs like alcoholics anonymous. As you probably know, they are the most common self-help groups in this country, and 10 percent of all Americans will go to an Alcoholics Anonymous (AA) meeting at least once in their lifetime (McCrady and Miller 1993). AA is the largest of the 12-step fellowships. Although based on some Christian teachings, 12-step programs draw the distinction between being religious and spiritual. They claim to be spiritual, not religious, in their approach to sobriety.

In 12-step programs a core spiritual belief is that there is a transcendent being or force that is referred to as a higher power. The definition of that being or force is a personal one. The crucial point is that the person seeking help must recognize that there is a power higher than him or herself to which to turn for guidance and wisdom. This higher power could be God, universal intelligence, or the wisdom of the 12-step group. People in these programs work on developing a personal relationship with a higher power and helping each other stay sober. They use prayer, meditation, and program strategies such as the 12 steps and 12 traditions. They usually believe in miracles and the mystical. The miracle of sobriety and other blessings are celebrated with humility and gratitude. Living in the moment, one day at a time, means the spiritual connection is constantly renewed. A commitment to make amends for wrongdoings is an ongoing part of the program. In addition, giving service to others is essential (Tonigan and Toscova 1999).

Do you identify with any of these 12-step beliefs? Which ones are familiar to you? Have you, or someone close to you, ever been involved in a 12-step program? If so, what impact has that had on your life or on the life of those you know? Take some time to write about this in your journal. You may want to refer to it later.

Belief in God

According to recent surveys, 95 percent of Americans believe in God and 90 percent say that they pray or meditate. Over 70 percent of Americans believe in life after death and 82 percent believe that God performs miracles. In addition, over 50 percent of the people surveyed believed that they had a sudden religious experience or religious insight within their lifetimes (Hamer 2004).

What does God mean to you? Is God a supernatural being? Is God another name for the personification of love or the creative spirit? Is it a life force with which you align? Soon we will ask you to write a spiritual autobiography so, in preparation, please write in your journal what the word and concept of God means to you.

In a previous book, we wrote about some exercises that have been helpful to our clients who are interested in clarifying their spiritual beliefs (Hoffman and Hoffman 1998). This process may be helpful to you as well. In your journal, list the heroes you had as a child. They may be characters from history, religion, books, comics, television, movies, or people you actually knew (family or friends.) Write the name of each hero and a few words about why this person was special to you. Also indicate if you still hold this person in such high esteem.

Next, write a description of the "God" you believed in as a child. Was that God like your childhood hero, or was it more like someone you feared? Sometimes it helps to use drawing instead of words to express concepts that do not translate easily into language. While it may sound childish, please bear with us as we ask you to make some drawings in your journal. First, draw a picture of you as a child and your childhood conception of God. Now, draw a picture of you and your concept of God today. How are they different? How are they the same? Please write about your thoughts and feelings as you worked on these drawings.

In our clinical practice, we have found several reasons that clients reject not just the belief in God but any connection with spirituality. Some people may believe that science is not compatible with religion. Perhaps they prayed to God in a time of need. When their prayers were not answered the way they wanted, they stopped believing in God. They may be angry and blame God for not protecting them and meeting their needs. Chemically dependent or very depressed people may be unable to feel any connection with the transcendent (Hoffman and Hoffman 1998). For these people and others who are willing to begin a spiritual program, we recommend some general spiritual practices. We have included these practices in the next chapter.

Ten Commandments

Most of us are familiar with the Ten Commandments that Moses brought down from Mt. Sinai. The first four religious commandments focus on our relationship to God: Have no other gods, do not use God's name in vain, do not worship idols, keep the Sabbath holy. Then there is a positive commandment: Honor your father and your mother. Finally, these five secular, legalistic prohibitions complete the set: Do not commit adultery, do not steal, do not kill, do not bear false witness against thy neighbor, do not covet your neighbor's possessions, including your neighbor's spouse.

These commandments are an historical benchmark and set forth fundamental rules for human conduct. How do you feel as you read them? Are they an integral part of your life? As you consider them, you may ask how following them can help you relate lovingly and compassionately to others. Take a few minutes to write in your journal. We will refer to this topic a little later as you prepare your spiritual autobiography.

The Five Mindfulness Trainings

According to Thich Nhat Hanh, the Five Mindfulness Trainings came from the Buddha (2003). While not commandments, they are commitments to help increase awareness of thoughts and actions. They are interrelated to all aspects of life. Awareness of our interdependence helps us maintain our compassion and an open heart.

The First Mindfulness Training is on the reverence for life. Reverence is the virtue that keeps us from acting like God (Woodruff 2001). This training cultivates compassion for all living things: human, plant, animal, and mineral. In our reverence for life, we vow not to kill or condone violence.

The Second Mindfulness Training is on generosity. We vow to be generous with our time, energy, and resources by extending them to those in need. We do not steal, possess the property of others, or profit from another's suffering.

The Third Mindfulness Training addresses sexual responsibility. We vow to act respectfully towards others and do not engage in sexual relationships without love and long-term commitment. We also honor the commitments of others and protect couples, families, and children from sexual misconduct.

The Fourth Mindfulness Training focuses on deep listening and loving speech. We vow to speak the truth with love and respect for the purpose of inspiring joy, hope, and confidence. We know that suffering is caused by gossip and discord, so we make efforts to resolve conflicts and reconcile differences.

The Fifth Mindfulness Training addresses mindful consumption. This encourages mindful eating, drinking, and consuming. Proper diet of the mind and body are essential to transform ourselves. Damage to our bodies betrays our ancestors and our children. The focus of the fifth training is on transforming ourselves and our society by being careful about what we consume and how we consume.

Do these mindfulness trainings appear to be similar to some of the Ten Commandments in their focus and priorities? Do they reflect your personal beliefs? Again, it would be helpful to write in your journal about your thoughts and feelings. In your spiritual autobiography, you will bring together many thoughts that you have written about in your journal.

EXPERIENCES

Your personality characteristics may affect your religious experiences. Events that happen in your life, and the meaning you assign to them, also shape your spiritual life.

Religion and Personality

There are three personality dimensions that appear to be genetically influenced and biologically determined: the extent to which a person seeks novelty, how dependent the person is on external rewards, and how much the person wants to avoid harm by avoiding risks (Cloninger 1987). Someone who does not seek much novelty, enjoys being with others, and avoids taking big risks would be conservative, socially outgoing, and perhaps fearful and anxious. This personality structure may be drawn to traditional religions (Koenig 1994a). On the other hand, who would shy away from traditional religions? The research shows that people who seek novelty and are not particularly fearful may find traditional religions constricting and inhibiting (Boomsma et al. 1999). Of course, religion may also affect personality development by promoting some traits, such as finding pleasure in increasing social interaction. Other traits may be suppressed, such as high novelty seeking and low harm avoidance. In addition, some personality characteristics may change due to the passage of time and having various life experiences.

Where are you along these dimensions? Do you seek much novelty in your daily life? Is it important for you to have contact with others, and do you find it pleasant? Do you avoid experiences because you are fearful or anxious? Where you place yourself in this regard may indicate how likely you are to be comfortable in traditional religions. Please realize that any research just looks at trends and cannot predict what is true for everyone, so if this analysis doesn't fit you, don't be surprised.

Many personality characteristics have been studied, but several are of particular interest: hostility, optimism, and hope. Hostility, as you probably know, encompasses anger, mistrust, and resentment of others. People who score high in the area of hostility are likely to have an increased risk of coronary heart disease. Not surprisingly, religious involvement is associated with lower levels of anxiety, aggression, and hostility, as is the capacity to forgive. Optimism and hope go hand in hand, and we will look more closely at this connection in the next chapter. For now, it's enough to say that people who are optimistic expect good personal outcomes, and they tend to have better mental health. Religious involvement is associated with higher levels of optimism and hope, even for people experiencing high levels of stress.

Religious or Spiritual Experiences

Religious or spiritual experiences range from "born again" conversions to a more gradual coming to belief (Gilbert 2000). At some points in life, your religious or spiritual experiences may involve intense wonder and joy. These are called *peak experiences*. At other times you may feel a warm and comforting serenity. This is known as *plateau experience*. Or perhaps a tragic event has transformed your life. These are called *valley experiences*.

PEAK, PLATEAU, AND VALLEY EXPERIENCES

Peak experiences are available to all of us. You don't need to believe in a higher power to have them. A peak experience is ecstatic. It's a feeling of being a part of something greater than oneself (the cosmos, beauty, a cause greater than ourselves.) At these times, you may say to yourself: "This is why I came into the world—to experience this!"

A feeling of well-being characterizes plateau experiences. You have a sense of deep satisfaction and the pleasure of serenity. In this moment, you are able to accept things as they really are without having a need to change anything. You feel alive in the present, with no distractions of living in the past or projecting into the future.

Valley experiences may involve times of pain, suffering, and meaningless. You are without the ecstasy of the peak experience or the serenity of the plateau experience. Valley experiences take you down into the depths of darkness. Many of us do not have a clear sense of ourselves or what is meaningful to us until we pass through a valley experience (Palmer 2000).

We may not need significant religious experiences to thrive in adverse circumstances. Paul Pearsall wrote a book called *The Beethoven Factor: The Positive Psychology of Hardiness, Happiness, Healing and Hope* (2003). In it, he gives examples of people who appear to thrive in the face of adversity. They may or may not have spiritual experiences. Most of us know that Ludwig von Beethoven wrote beautiful music, including his Ninth Symphony, when he was deaf. What many of us do not know is that when Beethoven was thirty-one years old, he was poor, hopeless, and suicidal. How did he get from age thirty-one to fifty-six to write the Ninth Symphony, no longer suicidal but filled with energy and creativity? Beethoven appeared to thrive and meet life's challenges even as he was losing his hearing. He was an ordinary man who learned to cope by shifting his expectations to meet the reality of his life and find purpose and meaning in the process (Pearsall 2004).

Have religious or spiritual experiences shaped your life? If so, what were they? Was there a time that you were so low that you either lost or found your faith? Have you had peak experiences when you felt elated and you knew that you were connected to something larger than yourself? Were you in nature, with others, or alone when this occurred? Have you had times that are filled with serenity and a warm, loving sense of gratitude? Writing about these experiences will be useful when you write your spiritual autobiography.

SPIRITUAL DEVELOPMENT

Reverend Scotty McLennan, Unitarian Universalist minister and college chaplain, believes there are stages of spiritual development that may correspond to chronological age. James Fowler (1981) and others have also hypothesized that we pass through distinct stages in our spiritual quest for meaning. Here are the stages outlined by McLennan (1999), with the corresponding chronological ages and experience of God:

Stage	Age Range	Experience of God
Magic	2–10	All-powerful God
Reality	6+	Cause-and-effect God
Dependence	12+	Idealized parent God
Independence	16+	Distant God (or atheist)
Interdependence	Adult	Paradoxical God
Unity	Adult	All pervasive God

The Magic Stage occurs in the youngest years. Developmentally, everything in the world is magic at this age. There are basically two categories of people: heroes and villains. The world is full of spirits and demons. God can fight monsters and God makes everything happen.

After age six, we start to wonder if Santa is real. This is the Reality Stage. We start to think in terms of what is and what is not real. Scriptures seem true in a concrete sense. It seems that God can be influenced if we are "good." In the dependence stage, age twelve or older, we start to struggle with dependence and independence. This is when we may start to long for a personal relationship with God, who becomes our idealized parent. An important person may be responsible for shaping our faith at this time. At around sixteen years of age, we may move from religious to spiritual, as we may start to reject institutions, such as religion. This is the Independence Stage. Spiritual life becomes personal and unique. We may want to demystify scripture, and we may start to think of God as an impersonal force. Perhaps we start to think of God as nonexistent, and we may become atheists during this period.

In the Interdependence Stage, religious symbols become sacred again and spiritual awareness tempers critical analysis. A spiritual community becomes important to us, even as we maintain our distinctive faith. God can be both personal and an impersonal force. Finally, at the Unity Stage, we have deep relationships with people of different faiths and traditions. We can tolerate ambiguity and paradox. God is experienced as divine spirit in everything and everything exists in God.

Some people resent being categorized within these stages. It is important to remember that this is just a model, and it may have interest or use to you or it may not. Take what fits and leave the rest. In your journal, please record your reactions to this view of spiritual development. Can you see yourself in these stages of spiritual or religious development? Remember that you are preparing to write your spiritual autobiography, and the notes you make in your journal will help.

How do you go about finding your religion if the faith you had as a child has lost its meaning? McLennon (1999) offers suggestions to follow. Start to think about religion. Keep an active, inquiring attitude. Pick a path, something that intrigues and engages you. Then begin to walk that path. Join with fellow travelers on the path you've chosen. Being part of a religious community of like-minded people can enrich your experience. This can strengthen the path you have chosen.

Prayer is a part of many religions. There can be great power in prayer and meditation. These disciplines can help with fear of death, alienation from others, the experience of terrible pain, and the feeling that life is not worth living. Prayer and meditation can help you maintain a reverent attitude and relationship with the transcendent throughout life. This is hard to do if you've lost your spiritual connection. There is pain in life. Pain is inevitable, but the impact is not. Does the pain strengthen you or defeat you? Explore how different traditions explain pain and suffering. Discover what makes sense to you.

DON'T FORGET TO DANCE

Many take up spiritual practices because they have a longing: a longing for spontaneity, self-expression, and play. By nature, we long to be free. The arts can help. Song, poetry, and visual arts can transform your spiritual life. So can dance.

Nina Wise encourages us to dance for self-expression and spiritual practice (2002). This can be joyful and spirit-filled. If you dance in private, you will be more focused on your internal experience than on the reaction of others to your dance. Wise has several suggestions to help rediscover your body by focusing on movement. Use music that has a rhythm you can feel in your body. Be mindful, and focus on what you're doing. Feel what it's like to be in your body. Pay attention to even the smallest movement. Don't judge or critique your dance or your body. This can make you self-conscious and rigid. If you are awkward in your movement, go deeper into that experience until you come out the other side.

Gabrielle Roth believes that we can dance our prayers. Her video, *The Wave: Ecstatic Dance for Body and Soul* illustrates the point (1993). In it, there is a progression through a series of rhythms: flowing, staccato, chaos, and lyrical, gradually slowing into stillness, coming to rest and focusing on the dance within. What follows is an opportunity for reflection and insight.

SPIRITUAL WRITINGS

Here we include examples of spiritual writings from friends who express a wide diversity of religious experience and beliefs. Notice that they are different in format and design. As you review them, think about how your beliefs and experiences are similar, and different from the examples we present here. You may be stimulated to write more about your own spiritual experiences in your journal. If these writings stimulate other thoughts or feelings for you, add that to your journal, too.

Cynthia

I believe in the interdependent web of all existence, of which I am a part. I am not the center of the universe—I am just one part of nature and should treat all living things with reverence.

I strive to live in harmony with nature and not subjugate it or try to bend it to my will. I must do whatever I can to protect the environment and to support others who protect nature.

I believe that mankind has the capability to live in harmony with one another, and I must do whatever I can to foster understanding and harmony among people. I will respect the beliefs of other people as long as they do no harm. I will lend my voice and my support to those who undertake to build world peace and understanding.

I believe that mankind has created "God" while ignoring the perfection and synchronicity of nature, which is more worthy of our devotion—but not worship—than any god or goddess figure. I will strive to live the kind of life that will exemplify these ideals and confound others who believe that in order to be good you must believe in God.

I believe that death returns us to nature in our elements, and that our true legacy is in the impact of our ideas, our actions, and our contributions to the world. We also live on in our families and in the children who may or may not carry our genes, but certainly hold our memories in their hearts.

I believe in the power of love.

I believe that beauty and harmony are all around us, and that we should always be attentive and respectful to it.

Ruth

For me, God is a power, far greater than myself, found in the process of love and interaction. It is difficult for me to imagine a personal relationship with a process, so I choose to experience this higher power as a presence that is with me at all times to guide, love, and nurture me. My relationship with the higher power is the most important relationship of my life. As that connection goes, so goes my connection with the rest of the world. My spiritual faith is based on:

Connection to my soul, other people, community, art, and a higher power who is within us, among us, and beyond us.

Compassion for others and myself without harshness and judgment.

Contribution to others, to be of service to people and our planet.

Commitment to honor my obligations and responsibilities to myself and others.

Convictions, covenants, and ethics to guide my path with gratitude, compassion, and generosity to others.

In moments of decision, when faced with two options,
I commit to take the path that will lead to greater compassion
and love for my family and community.

Rex

I was raised in the post-war era, belonging to a Reform Jewish synagogue, which we attended twice a year. I went to religious school through my Bar Mitzvah and Confirmation. My parents' friends were all Jewish, but this seemed purely an ethnic identity. Being Jewish included presents on Hanukah, a special dinner (no prayers) on Passover, Jewish chauvinism, and a constant vigilance for anti-Semitism. In nine years of religious school, I learned to read (but not understand) Hebrew and learned several bible stories and rituals, but I had no sense of Judaism as a moral guide or way to reach a higher level of living or being.

My Jewish identity has remained surprisingly important to me and has helped me connect with people of other faiths, especially Catholics. I am fascinated by diversity, ethnic and religious, and the evolution of these identities through generations.

I belong to a Reform Synagogue. Every year on the High Holidays my wife and I discuss how nice it would be to attend services more, but we rarely do. Reform Judaism is a comfortable place for my explorations into the questions of what, if any, meaning our lives have. Two of my favorite sources are Victor Frankl and Harold Kushner.

I believe that whatever God is, God isn't that which other humans, with certitude, tell us. I have recently begun, as a layperson, to glimpse at physicists' and astronomers' concepts of the universe. This has convinced me that I cannot come close to getting my mind around some basic concepts such as the beginning (or timelessness) of the universe or its immensity. If God is greater than the universe, how can I (or my fellow humans) hope to understand God? Therefore, I reject almost all concrete renditions of what God is and those who seem to know what God wants of us.

I believe that through the centuries we have used the word "God" (and many others) to try to understand the meaning of life, because it is unbearable for us to think that we have no meaning or purpose. Concepts of God differ among cultures and evolve as our scientific knowledge increases. Yet the moral underpinnings of these beliefs, over time and between cultures, are remarkably similar.

I believe that every phenomenon in the world can probably be explained in numerous ways. Love can be described entirely by stimulus-response deterministic psychology, by brain chemistry and atomic physics, by fundamental Christianity, or by Greek mythology. When we experience love or hope, behave courageously or altruistically, or in other ways transcend our selfish and base interests, then I experience God. In Les Miserables Victor Hugo says "to love another person is to see the face of God." I agree.

Beth

The chapter headings in my spiritual autobiography are hymn titles that were central to my spiritual life growing up in a United Methodist family where Mother played the piano, Daddy sang bass, and my two sisters and I would gather 'round the piano to sing along or to play our musical instruments.

Chapter 1: Early childhood, "Jesus Loves Me, This I Know"

Chapter 2: Ages 10–16, "How Firm a Foundation"

Chapter 3: Ages 16–18, "A Charge to Keep I Have"

Chapter 4: Ages 18–25, "Blest Be the Tie That Binds" or "I Love to Tell the Story"

Chapter 5: Ages 26–27, "I've Found a Friend"

Chapter 6: Ages 28–39, "Awake, Awake, to Love and Work"

Chapter 7: Ages 40–51, "How Can We Sing the Lord's Song in a Strange Land?"

Chapter 8: Ages 51–53, "I Know Not What the Future Hath"

Chapter 9: Age 53, "It Is Well with My Soul"

From Chapter 1: Early childhood, "Jesus Loves Me, This I Know" As children, we were protected from the harsher realities of the world that impact on many children's lives: domestic violence, chemical addiction, unemployment, poverty, hunger, and war. We grew up trusting and experiencing that we were loved and would be cared for. Back then, we didn't know to use the phrase, WWJD, ("What would Jesus do?"), but we were taught that he was the model we should follow to lead our lives.

From Chapter 5: Ages 26–27, "I've Found a Friend" The hymn tells of finding Jesus as a friend for life. The friend I found was my life partner, May—a woman—twenty years older than I, divorced, with four children. "Coming out" to ourselves, our families, and over time to our communities led me on a spiritual journey: first, out of pastoral ministry; then, out of church participation and away from organized religion.

From Chapter 7: Ages 40–51: "How Can We Sing the Lord's Song in a Strange Land?" What began as an angry exile from the church ended in a contented, productive distance in mid-life, full of rich relationships and continued growth and learning. I was quite at home in the secular world, but everywhere around me I encountered the sacred and I knew I was still in exile—not welcome in my native land.

From Chapter 10: Age 53, "It Is Well with My Soul" On July 25, 2004, *I walked into a Unitarian Universalist church. Within minutes of the service's start, I was filled with a peace and joy unparalleled in many years. I had found a new, welcoming spiritual community, I was home. A few months later, after signing the membership book and joining the choir, I choked back tears as I sang with the choir, "It is well, it is well, with my soul." It is, indeed, now well with my soul.*

YOUR SPIRITUAL AUTOBIOGRAPHY

Each of us has a rich and complex story to tell about our experience with spirituality. What is yours? Your spiritual narrative is unique. Writing your spiritual autobiography can help crystallize your understanding of what is important to you in life. Author Richard S. Gilbert proposes a model that we have adapted (2000). When you complete these exercises, your story will unfold, and you may be surprised at the clarity you receive. Don't feel you have to rush. Take your time, and be mindful of your thoughts and feelings. Now, take a few deep breaths and move through the next section as it guides you to write your spiritual autobiography. You will notice that what you have focused on has become a significant part of your life.

Your first step is to construct a time line:

1. Draw a vertical line on a long piece of paper.

2. Put a dot at the top of the line. Mark it "Birth."

3. Put a dot at the bottom of the line. Mark it "Death."

4. Put a dot somewhere along the line to signify the current time. Mark it "Now."

Stop for a moment and reflect on how you feel when you look at the time line: birth, death, and where you are now. In your journal, make a note of your thoughts and feelings.

1. Along the time line, note several significant life events that shaped your spiritual life.

2. Now, place three or four significant people on the line who had an impact on your spiritual journey.

3. Note any significant communities (religious or not) of which you or your family were/are a part.

4. Note on the line any significant spiritual or religious experiences you have had: peak, plateau, and valley.

Now that your time line is defined, use it as a base to write your spiritual autobiography in narrative form. Start with the items on your time line. Also, you may want to include some of the information you've already written in your journal. For example, include your experiences with prayer and meditation. How has your conception of God or a higher power changed since childhood, if at all? Write about your beliefs and moral code. Finally, complete your autobiography with a brief summary statement about yourself that you would like to have on your tombstone. How would you like to be remembered at your funeral or memorial service?

We suggest that you do not rush ahead in this book until you take some time to begin writing your spiritual autobiography. It will be rich and filled with the substance of your life experiences. Focus your attention on where you are in your journey now. Consider how your beliefs and practices reflect the meaningful activities in your blueprint. Please give yourself this gift of insight and write in your journal about this. It will sharpen your awareness and increase your motivation to live a more focused life if you take the time to make these connections.

Chapter 5

Quality of Life

Spirit of life, come unto me.
Sing in my heart all the stirrings of compassion.
Blow in the wind, rise in the sea;
move in the hand, giving life the shape of justice.
Roots hold me close; wings set me free.
Spirit of life, come to me, come to me.

—Carolyn McDade*

What you focus on becomes your life. This is a central idea running throughout this book. But what if you are faced with problems that directly interfere with the quality of your life that you can't simply overcome through better management of your attention? In this

* Reprinted by permission of the Unitarian Universalist Association

section, we will review the major domains that comprise what we think of as quality of life. For each domain we will encourage you to list problem areas you wish to consider. We will also examine practices to enhance well-being, including forgiveness, optimism, hope, and gratitude.

We suggest that as you review this section, you keep in mind "The Serenity Prayer" attributed to theologian Dr. Reinhold Niebuhr.

> God, grant me the serenity
> To accept the things I cannot change,
> The courage to change the things I can,
> And the wisdom to know the difference.

There may be aspects of your life that are beyond your control to change, like a chronic health condition or a child's disability. For these things, we encourage acceptance and self-care. For the aspects of your life that you may be able to improve, we strongly encourage you to note them. In chapter 6 we will present a way of considering the idea of change, even when you're not yet ready to stop a harmful behavior or start a new, healthy one in order to live a more focused life.

COMPONENTS OF WELL-BEING

How good is your life right now? Philosophers have been trying to tackle this question for centuries. Social scientists still struggle to find a way to measure overall quality of life. The difficulty with this question is that it's really not just one question. There are many different facets of quality of life; therefore, the answer often depends upon who you ask. The World Health Organization has developed a tool to measure overall quality of life called the World Health Organization Quality of Life Assessment (WHOQOL Group 1995). The WHOQOL examines six domains that are suggested to comprise one's overall quality of life. As you read through them, think about these areas in your own life. As you do, make notes if there are areas that you might wish to address now or in the future. Also note any areas that you think you should address but have no intention of doing so. This activity will be of use in chapter 6.

Physical Well-Being

Do you experience physical pain or discomfort? Do you have enough energy, or do you easily fatigue? Are you able to function sexually? Are you able to sleep and do you awaken feeling well-rested? Do you experience difficulties with your vision, hearing, or other senses? If you have physical problems, are they being addressed adequately? If you have medical problems that you have not dealt with, doing so may be one way to significantly improve the quality of your life.

Do you misuse alcohol? Do you use tobacco? Do you use street drugs or abuse prescription medications? Since we may not be able to accurately assess these areas in our own lives, has a trusted friend or loved one ever expressed concern about any of these areas? If you struggle with an addiction, we suggest you seek help through Alcoholics Anonymous, Narcotics Anonymous, a drug and alcohol treatment provider, or a psychotherapist trained to deal with addictions.

In this country many of us do not have adequate health insurance or, for other reason, are unable to receive the appropriate medical care. However, there may be factors affecting our physical health that are more directly under our voluntary control. Many of us have the knowledge and tools to address our problem, but for a variety of reasons we choose not to do so. For example, we all know that regular exercise is good for us, yet how many of us actually do it consistently? In past work we considered some areas that fit under the heading of physical self-care (Hoffman and Hoffman 1998). We adapted them to include here:

- Maintain adequate nutrition with three meals daily and snacks as needed.

- Sleep six to eight hours each night.

- Exercise fifteen to twenty minutes a day, three times a week.

- Follow a daily personal-care routine.

- Abstain from tobacco and other drugs.

- Use only a minimum of sugar, caffeine, and alcohol.

- Balance work and leisure activities.

- Maintain regular physical and dental checkups.

Please take a moment now to record in your journal any areas of your physical well-being that you believe you are neglecting. Can you identify any obstacles to addressing the problem(s)? Remember, we're only looking for problems here that you have neglected to address fully. Please try not to place any value judgments on yourself. The purpose of this exercise is not to induce guilt, but to heighten awareness. After completing this exercise, put it away until we get to the next chapter.

Psychological Well-Being

This area is concerned with emotional well-being, self-esteem, and body image. Do you have difficulty experiencing positive emotions? Do you often feel down or blue? Do you have difficulty with your memory? Do you have adequate concentration? Many people needlessly neglect or even harm themselves psychologically. We encourage you to consider these areas of emotional self-care (Hoffman and Hoffman 1998).

- Avoid blame, self-pity, and self-righteousness.

- Avoid extremes and all-or-nothing thinking. Start aiming for the mid range.

- Recognize boundaries and maintain them.

- Remember that "No" is a complete sentence.

- Laugh and express joy. Play and have fun with friends.

- Practice mindfulness and stress-reduction techniques.

- Experience intimacy and tenderness in relationships with other people.

- Stop trying to control and fix others.

- Listen more. Give less advice and fewer explanations.

If you're struggling with significant emotional problems, we recommend that you seek an evaluation from your physician or from a licensed mental-health practitioner.

Please take a moment now to note any areas of your psychological well-being that you believe you are neglecting. Can you identify any obstacles to addressing the problem(s)? After completing this exercise in your journal, put it away until we get to the next chapter.

Level of Independence

This area concerns your functional ability to perform activities of daily living like bathing, dressing, grooming, cooking, and cleaning. Your level of independence with mobility, communication, and work are also included. If you're living a life in which all of your energy and attention is directed toward meeting basic needs, you will have little energy to focus on what else you want to do. For example, older adults who have a functional decline may decide to move out of a large house that requires a lot of upkeep and transition into an assisted-living facility. There, many of their more basic needs are taken care of by a trained staff. This can mean that the individual will have the energy to work on developing an important interest, like spirituality, in a way that was not possible before.

Please take a moment now to note any areas of your level of independence you can identify that you believe you are neglecting. Can you identify any obstacles to addressing the problem(s)? After completing this exercise in your journal, save it for the next chapter.

Social Relationships

The presence of a social support system can significantly influence your overall quality of life. Do you have people who are close to you? Do you have people who you can call on to help you physically or emotionally if needed? Are you part of a community of like-minded people with whom you can share ideas and feel connected? It is no surprise to us that most of the happiest people report having a rich and full social life (Seligman 2002). Many people are accustomed to living in relative isolation. Looking for opportunities to increase social contact, such as carpooling to work, can have a positive impact on overall life quality. Instead of simply attending church or a service-organization meeting, try volunteering to be on committee. Instead of eating lunch alone at work, make lunch dates with coworkers you enjoy. By adding small doses of socialization into your day, you can easily improve your life.

Please take a moment now to note any areas of your social relationships that you believe you are neglecting. Can you identify any obstacles to addressing the problem(s)? After writing in your journal, save it until we get to the next chapter.

Life Environment

Do you have physical shelter, safety, and security? How financially secure are you? Is your work satisfying? Do you have sufficient opportunities for recreation and leisure activities? Many people feel like they are just getting by. This can affect access to medical and psychological care, the ability to train for a meaningful career, and the ability to provide adequately for children and loved ones. Is it possible to adjust your lifestyle in a way that frees up money, time, or energy? Do monthly payments on that new truck keep you financially strapped? Do you need to have all of those TV channels if you can't afford to pay any more than the minimum monthly payment on your credit card? The big question is this: Are you making yourself more financially stressed and insecure in order to pay for the entertainment and "toys" that you really can't afford—and that consume most of your free time? Put more directly: *Are you working for nothing more than your distractions?* As you approach the end of your life, will you feel greater well-being and know what matters to you any more than you do today? If between now and then, you continue to fill your life with distractions, it's unlikely.

Please take a moment now to note any areas of your life environment that you believe you are neglecting. Can you identify any obstacles to addressing the problem(s)? Write in your journal in preparation for the next chapter.

Spirituality/Religion/Personal Beliefs

What we believe may be a key component to adding deeper understanding of the self and the universe. Many of these ideas were covered in the previous chapter, and you've probably written about them in your journal. Do you have a credo or system of ethical beliefs by which you live your life? Do you feel connected with something greater than yourself? Do you have a sense of meaning and purpose in your life? Religion and spirituality offer a way to conceptualize the world that can lead to greater feelings of well-being and contentment. A spiritual self-care list is included here (Hoffman and Hoffman 1998). Notice that attending religious services is only one of the nine suggestions.

- Acknowledge humility in not having the "right" answers.

- Laugh and express joy. Play and have fun.

- Enjoy art and music. Notice miracles in nature.

- Transform loneliness into quiet and peaceful solitude.

- Experience intimacy and tenderness in relationships with other people.

- Use the Serenity Prayer to experience a sense of well-being.

- Attend religious services, or spend time alone focusing on spiritual beliefs.

- Contribute time and talent to the community, in particular to those in need.

- Anonymously perform an act of kindness for someone.

Please take a moment now to consider the areas of your spiritual development you may be neglecting. Consult your journal for exercises in the previous chapter, then write about areas you are neglecting or barriers you are willing to address.

Right now you have an opportunity to change the course of the rest of your life, making it deeper and richer. This is your window of opportunity, a time when a focused awareness of a problem can be matched with your readiness to make a change. We will address this special time in more detail in chapter 6.

PRACTICES TO ENHANCE WELL-BEING

As you can see, your quality of life is related to virtually all aspects of living. Positive psychology instructs us that it is possible to have deficits in some areas of life, and still experience a high level of overall contentment and happiness (Seligman 2002). In other words, what you focus on becomes your life. The power of focus explains why a paraplegic person may experience a greater level of overall quality of life than a person with full physical functioning.

We have seen many people in our psychotherapy practice who have overcome tremendous hurdles and now live genuinely full and rich lives. Witnessing this has led us to remain doggedly optimistic that there is hope for everyone. We will say more on optimism soon, but first we'll turn our attention to forgiveness.

Forgiveness

We each have a finite number of moments on Earth. We don't know what that number is now, but when we reach the last one, what wouldn't we give for just a few more? In this light, how foolish it seems to waste time imagining getting even with the coworker who made the snide comment about your report, or the perfect retort you should have snapped back to the condescending maître d' in that fancy restaurant last night. For most of us, these relatively minor annoyances are usually not too hard to let go. On the other hand, it's obviously not as easy to forgive the drunk driver who killed your loved one in an automobile collision. But the sacrifice in your time and your physical and emotional health by not forgiving is real. You can't turn back the clock and stop the painful event from occurring; it is done. What you can do, with time and intention, is move toward forgiveness. (Forgiveness does not mean that you condone or forget the injustice you experienced.)

We include this section on forgiveness because most adults can identify at least one major hurt in their lives. Where a lack of forgiveness lurks, your attempt to reign in your attention to what really matters may always be limited. What you focus on becomes your life, so doing work on forgiveness may be necessary to clarify your focus and improve your life.

Many Christian and Jewish religious teachings advise forgiveness. The general notion is that God can forgive us, so we need to forgive each other. Psalm 85:2–3 says, "You forgave the iniquity of your people and covered all their sins. You set aside your wrath and turned from your fierce anger."

Eastern traditions teach compassionate tolerance toward others and view hurtful actions as coming from ignorance of the human condition and ultimately as a part of the complex interwoven fabric of life (Sanderson and Linehan in Miller 2003). Forgiveness replaces holding grudges or feeling resentment, hostility, anger, and justification for retaliation and revenge. Forgiveness is adaptive in that it's linked to physical and emotional health benefits. It also frees us from negative attachments to others. However, reconciliation is not always healthy if it leads to revictimization. Forgiveness can be intrapersonal (within yourself), interpersonal (between you and someone else), or situational (between yourself and some outside event). All of the work of forgiving may be done solely in your mind and does not require reconciliation. Forgiveness can affect your thoughts, feelings, behavior, and motivation. It requires a willingness to let go of your right to resentment and judgment while fostering compassion, generosity, and maybe even love, even if those positive feelings seem undeserved. The process of forgiveness usually requires making a realistic appraisal of the harm that was done and acknowledging the perpetrator's responsibility. After this, freely choosing to cancel the debt is the next step. It is harder to forgive when you're obsessive, hostile, or depressed. Ruminating in anger about being wronged makes it very difficult to let go and get on with your life. You remain an emotional victim and prisoner to the perpetrator.

There are some compelling reasons to forgive. Research suggests real benefits for the forgiver. When you focus on how you were wronged or hurt and engage in fantasies of revenge, you trigger the stress response. Heart rate and blood pressure increase, your muscles tense, and you become primed to react. Living this way produces chronic stress, a condition associated with higher-than-average risk of physical and emotional illness. Forgiveness can actually improve health and overall quality of life. In one example, people with chronic pain reported lower levels of pain following an eight-week forgiveness meditation study conducted recently at Duke University (Harvard Women's Health Watch 2005).

HOW DO YOU FORGIVE?

One of the leading researchers of forgiveness is a psychologist named Everett Worthington (2001). Dr. Worthington has written about his own journey to forgiveness. On the morning of New Years Day in 1996, Dr. Worthington, already a noted authority on forgiveness, received a call that challenged him to rethink his theory. On that morning, he learned that his elderly mother had been brutally raped and murdered in her apartment. He succeeded in forgiving the perpetrators of this horrific crime through his approach to forgiveness, called REACH. The acronym outlines the program. The approach may appear overly simple, but it is not an easy or brief process to work through. The model is as follows:

- **R** stands for *recalling* the incident objectively—just the facts.

- **E** stands for *empathizing* with the perpetrator and trying to understand the point of view of the person who wronged you. Try to imagine the pain, fear, rage, or despair they must have experienced to cause them to lash out in an unthinking way. This isn't easy, but if you try to imagine a time when you thoughtlessly hurt someone else, you may gain some opening to understand how complex human motivation is.

- **A** stands for making an *altruistic* gift of forgiveness. Giving this gift makes the giver feel better. Don't get hung up on whether or not they deserve it. A reward is given to someone who deserves, a gift is given by someone who chooses to be kind regardless of the recipient's worthiness.

- **C** stands for *committing* to make a public statement of your forgiveness by writing it in a journal and telling a friend or a therapist.

- **H** stands for *holding* on to forgiveness. Though anger and vengeful feelings will come, it is this last step that will help you to return your focus to your choice to forgive. We don't choose to be victimized, but we can choose to forgive. This is a powerful difference between remaining a victim and moving on to become a survivor with a purpose in life.

Again, this is no easy task. You may not be able to forgive without the help of a minister or a therapist, and some people will have more difficulty forgiving than others. The type of wrong that was done will also affect how difficult it will be to forgive. An accident is easier to forgive than an intentional act, and an apology may also help to ease the way for forgiveness. Also, forgiveness is not a state; it is a skill and a practice. It takes time and intention to improve this ability, and it takes a moment-to-moment commitment to sustain (Sanderson and Linehan in Miller 2003).

HOPE AND OPTIMISM

At some point, all of us have felt a pull from the future—a desire to be more than we are today. When we expect good things to happen in the future, and we engage in activities to achieve our goals, we are hopeful, optimistic, and future-minded (Peterson and Seligman 2004). Being hopeful is an emotion. Being optimistic relates to expectations, and when we are future-minded, we think about the steps necessary to get from the present to our goals in the future.

We assume that you have had the expectation that you will have a "good" day. You expect things to go well, you have a plan of action, and you get busy to meet your goals. In this case, you have the feeling of hope, the expectation of success, and an understanding of the steps you need to take. During your day, you may have negative experiences at times, but you expect the good to outweigh the bad.

Strongly optimistic and hopeful people make the best out of any situation, and they expect that their desired outcomes will occur. They are energized and motivated to do what it takes to produce good results, and they seem to experience success in their lives. That is not to say that bad things don't happen to these people. They just have a way of finding the bright spots in difficult events, a skill that leaves them buoyed through life's ups and downs.

An Example

An optimistic friend told us this story. She described leaving Pittsburgh after picking up her son from college to bring him home for Christmas break. As they were motoring along on the Pennsylvania Turnpike, the car just stopped running. After coasting to the side of the road they tried unsuccessfully to restart the engine. They were essentially stranded in the middle of nowhere in an age before everyone had a cell phone. It was already almost dark on this Friday evening. They hiked the eighth of a mile back to the turnpike callbox to seek help. They called a towing company, then they called a friend from Harrisburg to come and get them. The car was towed to a service station in the nearby small town. But the garage was closed for the weekend, and the only place to wait for their friend was in an adjacent convenience store.

Instead of feeling frustrated about the delay and an unexpected car-repair bill, the two spent the evening talking with each other and with a pleasant and sympathetic store clerk in a store with few customers. They described the time as an unexpected, unscheduled time to catch up on life. The clerk made them as comfortable as possible and treated them kindly. By the time their ride came, the two had befriended the clerk. In an act of gratitude for the clerk's hospitality, the friend purchased a greeting card in the store and wrote her a heartfelt note of thanks. The clerk was so moved by the gesture that her eyes filled with tears. She said that encounters with people like them, rare as they may be, made her work enjoyable. The experience turned out to be one of the highlights of the holiday, and years later, our friend still recalls the story with fondness. Even though plans were unexpectedly altered, the desire to have a pleasant time was greater than the inconvenience. It turned out to be an enjoyable experience. Our friend also expressed relief and gratitude that the car stopped when it did instead of during a storm or in a highly congested expressway.

If you're an optimistic person, you may identify with this story. If not, you may wish you could be more like our friend. Contrary to popular myths, most people can become more optimistic if they take the necessary steps. There are a variety of methods to achieve this goal. Some of the most widely applied methods involve cognitive-behavioral therapy, in which an individual learns to recognize and correct self-defeating thoughts as they arise. We will talk more about that soon.

For now, just remember that when you're optimistic and hopeful, you are in good company. People who are optimistic and hopeful experience less depression and fewer physical problems. They are more resilient when faced with significant stress, and they probably have greater longevity (Koenig et al 2001).

Hope

People who are more religiously devout tend to be more hopeful (Sethi and Seligman 1994). This topic has been explored with a variety of religious affiliations and religion appears to be a source of comfort and hope (Koenig et al 2001). In one study, researchers divided nine religions into three categories. Orthodox Judaism, Islam, and Calvinism were considered to be fundamentalist religions. Catholicism, conservative Judaism, Lutheranism, and Methodism were considered to be moderate. Unitarian Universalism and reform Judaism were categorized as liberal religions. The fundamentalists reported a greater religious influence, religious involvement, and religious hope and optimism in their daily lives than people with moderate and liberal religious affiliations. The stronger focus on hope and optimism in fundamentalist materials and sermons may explain some of the differences. There was a moderate focus of hope and optimism in the moderate religious groups. The least amount of hope and optimism appeared in the religious materials and sermons of the liberal religions (Sethi and Seligman 1993,1994).

Clearly there is a connection between religious beliefs and a sense of hope and optimism. When there is a belief in the supernatural and miracles, there seems to be greater hope and optimism (Koenig et al 2001). However, it's also true that, regardless of our religious beliefs, we tend to be more optimistic and hopeful when we have a sense of meaning and purpose in our lives (Koenig et al 2001). Therefore, people who do not adopt a strong religious emphasis may still experience hope and optimism when they are focused on living a secular life of meaning and purpose.

The lack of hope is what we call despair and hopelessness. Hopelessness is associated with depression and physical illness (Koenig et al 2001). In 1996, researchers in Finland conducted a long-term study with a large number of men to examine the relationship between hopelessness and death from cancer and heart disease (Everson et al. 1996). The men who felt hopeless died sooner than those who were not hopeless. Even men who didn't have a history of cancer or heart disease died sooner when they felt hopeless.

Optimism

People who are optimistic believe the bad things that happen to them are exceptions. They see negative incidents as unstable (not permanent), external (coming from outside themselves), and having a specific cause (Peterson and Seligman 2004). For example, a friend of ours got a bad grade on a test. This was her optimistic reaction:

The teacher asked questions that came from his lesson last Thursday, which I missed. Since I hadn't gone to class or gotten the notes for that day from a classmate, I did poorly on the test. When I study the material that I'm tested on, I do reasonably well. Next time I'll be sure to have the appropriate notes to study.

On the other hand, if we believe that the situation is stable and internal (not likely to change and stemming from us) and that we can't take action to make things better, we may feel helpless and depressed. Seligman developed a model of "learned helplessness" that has been valuable to therapists in working with clients (Seligman 1975). This is an example of another, less-optimistic friend's thinking:

The course is difficult, and I'm just not smart enough to pass the tests. It doesn't really matter how much time I put in, I always study the wrong stuff and end up with a failing grade. Why do I even bother going to class? It doesn't make any difference anyway.

To clarify our understanding of an optimistic style, we will look more closely at three dimensions of a person's *explanatory style* (the way one explains life events to oneself) that influence their level of optimism (Seligman 1991). The three dimensions Seligman specified are permanence, pervasiveness, and personalization. Not only can an individual's level of optimism be tested, it can also be changed. Let's take a look at these dimensions.

This first dimension measures how permanent you believe both good and bad events are in your life. People who believe that bad events are temporary and good events are permanent are more optimistic. On the other hand, those who see bad events as being more permanent and good events more temporary are more pessimistic. When you stop and think about it, this makes sense doesn't it?

The second dimension deals with how universal or specific the event is. People who believe that experiencing a bad event bodes ill for everything else in their life are more pessimistic. People who are able to confine a bad event to one area of life, not allowing it to affect other aspects of life, are more optimistic. On the other hand, when something good happens in one area of life those who see this as limited to just one area are more pessimistic. People who see a good event in one area of life as representing good things in all aspects of life are more optimistic.

Finally, people who blame themselves for bad events have lower self-esteem. Low self-esteem in this area is marked by internalizing bad fortune and externalizing good fortune. On the other hand, those who blame others for bad events and take credit for good events appear to have higher self-esteem.

If you were to get a failing grade on a test, how would you explain it? What about other failures in your life, how do you explain them? Take a few minutes and consider how you explain to yourself the reasons for not meeting your goals. Now write in your journal about your thoughts and feelings.

It's possible to change your explanatory style. You can boast your sense of positivity by noticing what you are telling yourself about events in your life and then bringing your thoughts in line with explanations that promote higher levels of optimism and self-esteem. To learn more about this topic, we refer you to the interesting work of Martin Seligman (you can find titles in the references at the end of this book). If you struggle with anxiety or depression, you may be interested in seeing a therapist to work on increasing your optimism.

It should be noted that more optimistic people are generally happier with themselves and life. They tend to be more creative, generous, and tolerant (Seligman 2002). However, they may be slightly less accurate judges of their own talents, looks, intelligence, and skills than their more pessimistic counterparts (Seligman 1991).

Improving Hope and Optimism

There is a growing body of research looking at how prayer and meditation affect one's mood and sense of well-being. The previous chapter reviewed much of this research, but here we want to discuss in some detail an important study that produced compelling findings in the area of optimism and hope. It was published in the journal *Psychosomatic Medicine,* and it was conducted by a team lead by Richard Davidson, Ph.D., Director of the Laboratory for Affective Neuroscience at the University of Wisconsin (Davidson et al. 2003). The study showed that people who are emotionally distressed, depressed, anxious, or angry have more activity in the right prefrontal cortex. This region of the brain is also associated with intense vigilance often seen in highly stressed individuals. When people are experiencing more positive emotions like joy, happiness, or optimism, there is increased activity in the *left* prefrontal cortex. By reading a baseline level of brain activity, the researchers were able to establish neural set points for each individual's moods. Most people are in the middle, with the ability to experience a mix of good and bad moods. The people on the far right are highly stressed, often depressed individuals. On the far left are the doggedly optimistic folks. A study was conducted to determine whether the set point for baseline mood could be altered through the daily practice of meditation, a practice widely used in many religious traditions.

The subjects in the study were highly stressed workers in a Wisconsin biotech company. The treatment group was provided with two months of mindfulness meditation training. Each participant meditated for one hour, six days per week for two months. The control group received no training. At the end of the study, the meditating group had shifted the baseline set point significantly to the left and had boosted their immune systems. The control group had no difference in either measure. Studies like this suggest that there is a measurable emotional boost that comes from practicing this discipline. There may also be a physical health benefit.

But there is a risk in assuming that we can totally control our health by applying spiritual or secular methodologies. A positive mental attitude may improve your health and mood, but it hasn't been demonstrated to cure or prevent serious illness like cancer. We include this cautionary statement because there is a risk of blaming ourselves for illnesses.

We believe that the best method for improving a sense of hope and optimism may involve mindfulness practice and/or religious or other spiritual practices, combined with a cognitive behavioral program of identifying and correcting negative beliefs about the future. We cannot predict the future, and therefore expecting negative future events is irrational. Expecting neutral or positive future events and then looking for them while moving beyond disappointments makes sense. This mindset improves your mood, increases your awareness of positive events when they do occur, and helps you to minimize downturns.

GRATITUDE

The quality of your life can be improved by paying attention to the small things that go well. Even negative experiences can be seen as gifts. Can you remember a time when a problem required you to stretch beyond your normal limitations? In the last chapter we talked about "valley" spiritual experiences. If you have not done this yet, recall how a valley experience changed you, and then write about that in your journal. Thoughtful self-reflection can be beneficial. Is there an insight from your valley experience for which you feel grateful?

Practicing gratitude is like starting to exercise a muscle (Napier 1997). At first, it seems difficult but, with practice, you establish a new routine and habit. You will notice that the more you focus on gratitude, the more things you find to be grateful for.

When you awakened this morning, what were your first thoughts? Were you mindful of opening your eyes to see the sun streaming in the window? As you got ready for work, where was your attention? Did you enjoy your morning shower as you smelled the scent of the shampoo and soap? Were you invigorated by the feeling of the brush moving along your scalp, bringing order to thousands of strands of hair with each pass? At the breakfast table, were you able to savor your first bite of food? Did you reflect with interest and surprise as you reviewed your dreams on the way to the office? Did you give thanks to a higher power or another source for the gifts you have today? Was your heart filled with warmth and gratitude? If you focused on being mindful and grateful, how did that feel? If you focused on negative thoughts, how did *that* feel? It is probably getting clearer to you that your focus becomes your life.

Let's take a closer look at gratitude. It means graciousness and relates to kindness, generosity, and gifts received. The feeling of gratitude is often experienced as appreciation and a sense of wonder. It is a pleasant experience, connected to contentment, hope, and happiness.

Gratitude can be extended to a higher power, to other people, to nature, to an organization, or to an idea. Self-satisfaction for the fruits of one's own hard work is not considered gratitude. Generally, there are three parts to gratitude: a warm appreciation, a sense of good will, and an inclination to act positively as a result (Fitzgerald 1998).

Historically, gratitude is highly valued as a virtue. This is true in Christian, Jewish, Hindu, Muslim, and Buddhist thought. When done with feeling, the practice of giving thanks before meals may be an important way to mindfully acknowledge how dependent we are on what we receive from a higher power, from friends and strangers, from nature, and from each other's good deeds.

We may be able to increase our grateful disposition in several ways: Increase the intensity of the gratitude (How mindful are we of the strength of our feelings of gratitude?); increase the frequency of feeling gratitude (How often do we feel grateful?); increase the span of our gratitude (In what areas do we feel grateful? Are we grateful for family, friends, and experiences in the past, opportunities for the future, blessings of health? For what else do you feel grateful?); and increase the density of our gratitude (For how many people do we feel grateful: friends, teachers, mentors, students, higher power?).

Dr. Robert A. Emmons and Dr. Michael McCullough collaborated in a long-term research project that collected scientific data on the causes and consequences of gratitude. The Research Project on Gratitude and Forgiveness produced some interesting information on the topic of gratitude. The Project explored effective ways to incorporate gratitude into daily activities and measured how people differ in their disposition for gratitude.

One way of increasing gratitude overall is to keep a section in your journal entitled "Gratitude." Research has shown that when people keep gratitude journals, they are more optimistic, feel better about their lives, and feel better physically. They even exercise more frequently (Emmons et al. 2000). As a matter of fact, when people in one study made daily instead of weekly entries of gratitude they had even higher levels of energy, alertness, enthusiasm, attentiveness, and determination (Emmons et al. 2003). In addition, when the people who kept daily records of gratitude were compared with people who kept records of problems and neutral events, the people who recorded their gratitude showed better attentiveness and alertness (focus) and higher energy (Emmons and McCullough 2003).

The research seems clear that when people feel grateful, they have more positive feelings. They are also more optimistic and less depressed. People who feel grateful tend to believe that we are all interconnected and they feel more committed to helping others. They are more likely to participate in spiritual or religious activities (McCullough et al. 2002). Finally, people who are grateful are less likely to be focused on material things, less envious of people with wealth, and more likely to share their resources with others. Soon, we will talk more about the connection between gratitude and generosity.

For many years, participants in 12-step programs have been encouraged to develop an "attitude of gratitude." This is particularly helpful for people who are indulging in self-pity and blaming others. It's difficult to feel sorry for yourself and blame others at the same time that you're feeling grateful. Try this yourself. You will see that these are opposite states of mind (just as you cannot be anxious and relaxed at the same time). The next time that you are in a "poor me" or "it's somebody else's fault" state of mind, start counting your blessings and feeling grateful. We think you will find this helpful. We have personal and professional experience of this being a powerful strategy to sharpen a focus on the present moment and what really matters in life.

There are big differences between feeling indebted to someone and feeling grateful. Think about this for a moment. Write in your journal about how feeling grateful differs from feeling like you owe someone something. Perhaps your experience is consistent with the research that shows that people who feel grateful have lower levels of anger and higher levels of love, happiness, and appreciation for others than people who feel indebted. Also, when someone feels that they're indebted to someone, they are less likely to want to spend time with that person than someone who feels grateful toward that person. Has that been your experience, too? Think about this and write your reflections in your journal.

Cultivating an attitude of gratitude is helpful to ourselves and to others. The more frequently we feel grateful, the more likely we should be able to overcome barriers that distract us from our focus on living a life of meaning. Some of these barriers include self-pity, blaming others, feeling envious, and focusing on the negative. So how will you use this information about the value of gratitude? In your journal, write about how feeling grateful can improve your focus on what is meaningful in your life. Please take a little time to do that now. We suggest that you pause and make a list of things, people, and opportunities for which you feel grateful. Notice how you feel when you have listed as many items as you can. You may want to make a note in your journal about how making the list made you feel.

Gratitude and Generosity

Grateful people are more empathic and understanding of others. Their friends and associates see them as generous and helpful (McCullough et al 2002). Gratitude and generosity are two sides of the same coin, since both attributes reflect the mind-set of abundance (Napier 1997). This way of looking at the world includes the belief that there is plenty to go around. It is the opposite of the belief that the world is a place of scarcity, in which you must hold on to everything you have since there will never be enough. The beliefs of abundance and scarcity have little to do with objective reality. People who have little money can be generous and people who are wealthy can hold on to every penny. In a similar fashion, you will find poor people who are grateful and wealthy people who are not. We have noticed that grateful people tend to be generous and people who are not grateful tend to be stingy. Have you noticed this to be true?

The spirit of generosity extends to all resources, not just money. For example, we may have time that we could give to a friend. We may have clothing that we could give to a shelter. We may have flowers in our garden that we could take to a sick neighbor. We may make an extra helping and invite a lonely person to dinner. During the past week, did you do anything generous with your resources? Give yourself some time to think about this. In your journal, write about ways you were generous with your resources and how it felt for you. Were you grateful that you had the resources to share? Consider writing in your journal about how gratitude and generosity are connected for you. Also, make a list of ways that you can be generous during the next week. When you do those things, be mindful about how it feels to you. It is also helpful to focus on the gratitude you have for these opportunities to be generous.

PRACTICE WHAT YOU PREACH

To illustrate the practice of forgiveness and gratitude, here is a story told by a therapist friend about a difficult situation he was going through at work. He was carrying around a lot of stress, resentment, and anger about a management decision to lay off several of his colleagues in his small department. Struggling to cope, he felt victimized and helpless. Although he realized there was nothing he could do to change the situation, he was ready and able to point out the problems with the layoffs and complain to those who shared his feelings. But this only made him feel worse. These bad feelings could be held at bay but were always just under the surface, ready to leap forward in the right setting. Nothing changed except that he made himself feel more stressed and angry, which was starting to take a toll on his physical and emotional well-being. He was stuck in his inability to forgive those who made the decision to let his colleagues go.

As a psychotherapist, he was spending his days counseling his clients on the practical and rational benefits of changing what they can and accepting what they cannot change. Yet he was struggling to practice what he preached and felt disingenuous. Was it that he didn't really believe what he told so many of his clients? No. He needed only to look at the volumes of scientific research and observe his courageous clients, overcoming major life challenges, to find all the evidence he needed to support the efficacy of his therapeutic interventions. What was the disconnect, then?

He was surprised to realize that he was ambivalent about letting go of his resentment. One part of him actually enjoyed the complaining and anger. It felt mood altering when he ranted on and on. It was tough to face, but a part of him actually liked to complain. He was clearly stuck in deep resistance of forgiveness. While he was criticizing the administration with his coworkers, he gained some immediate benefit in that he experienced a sense of solidarity with other disgruntled employees. This felt good. Unfortunately, the cumulative effect of commiserating was unhealthy for all involved. He also later noted that he derived some sense of control through the complaining, although this modest perceived benefit came with a significant downside—he was feeling pessimistic about his career and was unable to focus on anything about which to feel grateful. Any potential relief about still having a job was overshadowed by the negativity of self-pity and blaming.

The other, healthier part of him knew that by letting go of his anger and forgiving, he would have more energy to face the issues at hand, making them more manageable. He also knew that by letting this situation keep him stuck in anger, he was giving up control over his mood to the situation. He didn't like the idea of that at all!

As a therapist, he recognized that he had to acknowledge his mixed feelings and make a decision about what he should choose to focus on if he ever hoped to move on. Through the use of the technique to resolve his mixed feelings, (described in chapter 6) he was able to work through his ambivalence.

Our friend resolved his thoughts and feelings and found that he could accept things as they stood. With a moment-to-moment commitment to that decision and a long-range goal of being at peace with what he could not control, he was able to stop complaining and feeling sorry for himself. It was then that he realized that this experience helped him to become more aware of his own motivations and had ultimately helped him to become a better therapist. He needed to step back from the heat of his anger to find some meaning in the experience. Now he feels grateful for his insights, as they have contributed to his own personal and professional development. Our friend is hopeful and recognizes that whatever happens in his career, he will ultimately be okay. This story illustrates the power of working towards acceptance and finding gratitude for life's lessons, even those we don't see as lessons at first. We encourage you to stay tuned to the gifts that you receive each day, and to discover the gifts in disguise, like the story illustrates.

This same therapist has a long morning commute. He dedicates his forty-minute morning drive to prayer (with his eyes open!) and counting his blessings. He arrives at work feeling centered and energized. Our friend used to listen to the news on the way to work, which tended to focus his attention on his powerlessness in the face of the tragedies of the world. When he discovered that the useful information in the morning news reports was usually overshadowed by useless and frequently disturbing reports, it was an easy choice to turn off the radio and focus on what really matters to him. Our friend still keeps up with current events. He volunteers in service projects, changing what he can and making a contribution to his community. But he keeps that morning driving time for himself. It centers him for the day as he creates a mind-set of peace and gratitude, living in the present moment. We think this a good example of how a busy person found forty minutes each day to do something for himself. It had a significant positive effect on the quality of his life.

Consider your quality of life. How are you functioning in the areas we reviewed in this chapter? Are there areas that you want to improve? Are you able to identify any barriers or sources of your resistance? Spend a few minutes tuning into yourself, then write in your journal any ideas that arise. In the next chapter we'll help you to develop a personal focus plan to meet some of your goals.

Chapter 6

Personal Plan for Focused Awareness

The first of January is another dawning, the sun rising as the sun
always rises, the earth moving in its rhythms,
With or without our calendars to name a certain day as
the day of new beginning, separating the old from the new.
So it is: everything is the same, bound into its history,
as we ourselves are bound.
Yet also we stand at a threshold, the new year something
truly new, still unformed, leaving a stunning power in our hands.
What shall we do with this great gift of Time, this year?

—Excerpt from "New Year's Day"
by Kathleen McTigue.*

* Reprinted by permission of the Unitarian Universalist Association

Every day is the beginning of the rest of your life. In a sense, every day is New Year's Day. There is no time like the present to take what you know and put it into action. That's what we'll do in this chapter. If you were to wake up tomorrow morning and something in your life could be different (something you had the power to change), what would you want it be? Pause now and think about that question. Consider what really matters to you. How would sharpening your focus help you take steps in the direction of the change you just imagined? Take some time to think about this. Then write in your journal.

In this chapter and throughout the book we ask you to answer the following questions: What change do you need to make to improve your focus? How can you develop and maintain motivation to incorporate focus-enhancing practices into your daily life? How can your clarity of focus improve the quality of your life and help you increase your sense of purpose and meaning?

Up to this point we have reviewed what it means to live a life focused on what is important to you. We suggest that before continuing, you review journal entries related to exercises you have completed in the course of reading this book. Review the exercises on mindfulness from chapter 2, meaningful activity from chapter 3, spiritual activity from chapter 4, and quality of life from chapter 5. In the process of examining your journal entries, you will probably find reassurance that there are areas in your life that work well. We also expect that you have identified some areas that may be improved. Perhaps you have already made some changes.

The emphasis throughout this book has been on learning to live a more focused, engaged, and proactive life. We encourage you to actively overcome the passivity that allows you to drift off course. Think of this chapter as training to better sail yourself through the seas of your life. If you don't take control over the tiller and sails, forces outside of you will determine your course. In other words, if you are not focusing your attention on what is really important to you, you're allowing other people and situations to guide your life.

Now let's put the insights you have gained so far, through this book and from your life experience, into an action plan. This is your chance to continue to add positive behaviors that will help you bring greater focus, meaning, and well-being to your life. For example, take a daily walk with your partner or spend a half-hour each evening reading to your children. Do a good deed for someone or make a gratitude list each day. Pray or meditate daily. It's also helpful to identify potential obstacles that can undermine your success with these new, focus-enhancing activities. The obstacles may include any way you passively donate your attention to outside forces—for example, the time consumed by watching television, surfing the Web, or fantasizing about purchasing some new car or gadget.

Aim to change one thing at a time. Start small and simply. Remember to take your time. Protect yourself from becoming over-whelmed if you've identified many items you wish to change. You don't need to completely remake your whole life right now. Define your goals, prioritize them in order of importance, and proceed in a step-by-step way. We suggest that you first read through this chapter to learn more about how change occurs. When you're finished, consider the changes that you feel most ready to make. Then read through the chapter again. This time, you'll identify your level of motivation and match it to the suggested strategy. This may sound complicated now, but it will get clearer when we start to use specific examples.

CHANGE AND FALSE HOPE

Change is complex. Author Stephen Covey explains that the development of a new positive habit requires knowledge, skill, and desire (1989). One must have the knowledge that the new behavior is beneficial; possess the ability and skill to use the behavior; and maintain the desire to begin and continue the new behavior. In the absence of any of these elements, attempts to bring about change will likely result in failure.

In our book, *Recovery from Smoking: Quitting with the 12-Step Process*, we emphasized the idea that quitting smoking is a process, not an event, and is far more complex than applying willpower alone (1998). Numerous studies on change show that many of us repeatedly fail at maintaining changes for very long. On average, we make the same New Year's resolution for five years before we're able to sustain the new behavior for more than six months (Polivy et al. 2002). With this strong track record for failure, it is a testament to our persistence that we continue to try.

We often make incorrect assumptions about our failures. Janet Polivy and C. Peter Herman of the University of Toronto have coined the term *false hope syndrome* (2002). This syndrome includes failure to make lasting changes combined with unrealistic expectations. Specifically, we tend to set unreachably high goals and discount the smaller changes that we may actually experience. Then we expect change to occur more quickly than is possible. We also expect change to be much easier than is reasonable. Finally, we expect that a single change will result in unrealistically drastic improvement to our lives. Instead of recognizing that our expectations are unrealistic, we tend to believe that we didn't try hard enough and that we'll try harder next time. Or we think the task was too difficult and that we'll try a different strategy next time. These attributions often perpetuate failure. In addition, we minimize our smaller (and more realistic) successes and undermine our motivation for continued attempts. So, what lessons can we learn from this?

First, Be Realistic

We suggest that, if you set your goal appropriately from the outset, you will stand a much greater chance of success. All of us must realize that, despite the prevailing notion among Americans that it's possible to succeed at anything if you just try hard enough, this is probably not true. Let's face it: we simply don't all have the aptitude, personality, or natural ability to do anything we may want. However, we can choose to realistically incorporate our interests and passions into a well-focused and more meaningful life. While you may never become an expert on mindfulness, for example, you may enjoy taking an adult enrichment class on meditation at a local community college. You will probably not reach the same level of expertise as Jon Kabat-Zinn or Thich Nhat Hanh, but that limitation doesn't need to prevent you from taking steps to enjoy a deeply focused life. You don't have to devote the majority of your life to study, meditation, or prayer in order to reap the real benefits of incorporating these or other focus-enhancing practices into your life.

Next, Be Patient

Do not expect your changes to happen overnight. Change is a process, not an event. The process, at times, can move at a painfully slow pace. This is the nature of change. There are no shortcuts. When people try to rush the process, they tend to fail, and these failed attempts undermine real change. Research conducted over the past twenty years by James O. Prochaska, John C. Norcross, and Carlo DiClemente has shed light on how people change. Soon we will discuss some of their research findings.

Be Persistent

Change is not easy. You will experience times when you believe that it is too hard to change. Remember that making changes occurs in steps—you just need to keep gradually moving in the desired direction (Prochaska et al. 2002). There are activities to help you make progress. When you feel like you are losing your way and becoming bogged down, review how far you have come and what you've learned so far.

Again, Be Realistic

Be realistic about the benefits you are likely to experience as a result of adding a new practice to increase your focus in your life. Hopefully, as you sharpen you focus, you will find it easier to see clearly what is important in your life and discern the necessary steps to move forward to your goal. Be cautious not to expect these focusing skills to immediately result in dramatic success in your relationships, career, health, or finances. In reality, you should notice a positive cumulative effect as you become more mindful and intentional in the choices that you make. While it's true that these choices may result in you spending more time and attention in meaningful activity, please do not set yourself up for disappointment if your life is not dramatically transformed. For now, a realistic goal would be for you to see more clearly what is important in your life and to sharpen your focus on how you spend your time and energy. You have probably made progress in this direction just by completing the exercises in previous chapters.

MAKE TIME FOR CHANGE

From your journaling so far, you're beginning to create a mental picture of the life you want to live. As you consider this, you begin to notice what changes in your present life are necessary in order to have the life you want. To prepare yourself to focus on what is truly important, you will probably require some free time and energy to make the needed changes. Where will you get the time to begin to add new focusing practices like mindful meditation or prayer in your daily life? It is through these practices that you gain more control over your attention. But when will you "have" the time? In our clinical experience, a common objection that our clients have to including a new and healthy practice into their life is that they just don't have the time. Most of us live busy lives. Have you ever made a careful accounting of exactly what you do with each of the twenty-four hours (or 1440 minutes) that we each get every day? When we give this self-monitoring exercise to our clients and ask them to account for all of their time for one week, often they are astonished by how much time they spend engaged in activities that are unimportant to them, their families, or their communities. For anyone who has tried to start a financial budget, you may have done a similar exercise in tracking where all of your money goes. When you realize how much is being wasted on things that you don't need, this heightened awareness can be a powerful motivator to change. Most people deliberate more carefully upon how to spend money than they do on how to use their most precious resources—time and attention.

If you are one who believes you don't have the time to begin a new practice, we recommend that you try this exercise. For one week, write down how you use every hour. Include everything for the week. We know this isn't easy. It takes real diligence and persistence. If you skip some time, don't stop doing the exercise. Just start recording again and continue keeping track.

When you complete this task, review it. Where are you spending your time? It's true we all need to sleep and some of us are lucky enough to sleep about eight hours per night. Most of us must work to support ourselves, and including commuting time, we figure ten hours per workday are devoted to work. How about the remaining six hours each work day? How much time do you spend procuring, preparing, and consuming food? How much time are you engaged with friends and loved ones? How much time is devoted to your physical and spiritual self-care? Now look at how much you are doing that may not be very important to you? How much TV do you watch? How much unnecessary shopping are you doing? How much mindless Internet surfing? How much time is being wasted, in total? It's time to see for yourself. You may photocopy and enlarge this chart or duplicate it in your journal.

My activities for the week of: _____

	Sunday	Monday	Tuesday	Wednesday	Thursday	Friday	Saturday
5:00 am							
6:00 am							
7:00 am							
8:00 am							
9:00 am							
10:00 am							
11:00 am							
12:00 pm							
1:00 pm							
2:00 pm							
3:00 pm							
4:00 pm							
5:00 pm							
6:00 pm							
7:00 pm							
8:00 pm							
9:00 pm							
10:00 pm							
11:00 pm							
12:00 am							
1:00 am							
2:00 am							
3:00 am							
4:00 am							

Now that you've completed this exercise, think about how much time each day your new practice will take. If you plan to begin a practice of mindful meditation or contemplative prayer, for example, you may decide that you will need thirty minutes each day.

Next, look at your chart of activities for the week. What are you doing for thirty minutes that you can forego? Remember, your focus becomes your life. What is worthy of your focus? Reality TV or Web surfing may be fun, but they are, by their nature, a distraction, and they prevent you from focusing on what is truly meaningful and important.

Thoughtful self-reflection can be uncomfortable. Some of you will have difficulty with this exercise because it will force you to look at dysfunctional behaviors that you may not be able to simply stop on your own. Some readers may have addictions to alcohol, drugs, pornography, gambling, spending, or living an artificial life in Internet chat rooms. If, despite your best efforts, you are unable to control this type of behavior, you may benefit from consulting with a licensed professional trained in the treatment of addictions. As a result of doing this exercise, you may see that you are wasting your precious time and attention.

SIX STAGES OF CHANGE

All major change actually occurs in a series of stages, and what follows is based in part on research about change (Prochaska et al. 2002). Many people make the mistake of attempting to take action to begin a new behavior or stop a dysfunctional one before they are truly ready. The result is the inevitable failure to maintain the change for long. Often this only reinforces a belief like: "I tried that, and it didn't work." It is easy to see how aborted attempts can undermine future attempts at changing.

You will probably be more successful in making a change when you understand the stages of change, identify which stage you are in with regard to your motivation and preparation, and then pick helpful strategies to achieve your desired goal. Within each stage, the objective is simply to progress to the next stage. Moving forward one stage at a time, you will stand the best chance for success in making and sustaining the desired change.

Read the following overview of the stages of change before you decide where you are in your own process of change. You will learn how to motivate yourself to continue making progress. By following the recommendations for each stage, you can see yourself move through all of the stages of change, eventually complete the process, and succeed in maintaining your change. There is no shortcut to making real and lasting change. But if you are intentional about it, it need not take forever, either.

This discussion could sound very academic unless we pick an actual behavior to change. For the sake of illustration, we chose the focus-enhancing behavior of meditating each day. Suppose you want to start daily meditation because you believe that practice will help you be more relaxed and focused. Further, you believe that with your improved focus, you will waste less time and pay more attention to activities and people that give your life meaning. Using this example of meditation, let's read through the descriptions of the stages of change. We begin the discussion of each stage with a quote you may identify with if you are currently in this stage.

Precontemplation

"I am not interested in sharpening my focus with daily meditation. I'm fine the way I am"

If you are in the *precontemplation* stage, you don't see any reason to meditate (or use any other focusing strategy) each day or you believe you cannot make the time or effort right now. If you think that you can't or don't want to start meditating now, you are likely to be in precontemplation. A person in this stage would not have a serious intention to make a change (starting to meditate) now or in the near future (Prochaska et al. 2002).

If you have no real intention to make any changes to improve your focus through meditation (or another focus-enhancing strategy) anytime soon, then we might guess that you were given this book by a well-meaning friend or perhaps a spouse who sees potential in you if you become more focused. First, we must commend you for reading this far. If you completed the exercises up to this point then additional kudos to you because you've already made important progress toward changing. If you are open to doing so, we encourage you to try th e following suggestions to examine your thoughts and feelings more thoroughly, even if you have no intention of changing now or in the near future.

REVIEW THE OPTIONS

Here's an idea that may be helpful. Remember that the scope of this book is on adding focus-enhancing behaviors to your life. Several examples of these were already identified, as listed below. As you review them, consider an aspect of yourself that you have neglected. If needed, go back to review the appropriate chapter in the book to refresh your memory. Select an area that would help you better direct your own attention toward what is important to you. If you're not willing to meditate daily, would you be interested in another re-focusing practice or something else from the list below?

1. Begin a new mindfulness practice (chapter 2).

2. Become proficient with refocusing strategies (chapter 2).

3. Rediscover a lost, but once meaningful, activity as reviewed in the "blueprint" exercise (chapter 3).

4. Intentionally simplify your life (chapter 3).

5. Begin a new spiritual practice, or work on developing your spirituality (chapter 4).

6. Work a program of recovery for an addiction (chapter 4).

7. Enhance some aspect of your overall quality of life (chapter 5).

In reality, through your reading and completion of some of the exercises in this book, you may be able to select one new behavior to begin at some point in the future. If you are struggling with this, seek input from others in your life. If this book was given to you or recommended by others, ask them why they thought you should read it. Try to hear this feedback with an objective ear. Consider the input you're given and see if you can acknowledge any truth in parts of it. Use this information to assist you in gaining some insight into how you may be able to grow. If you purchased this book for yourself, what was your motivation for doing so? Go back in your mind's eye and try to recall what you initially hoped to gain from reading this book. Because motivation for change wavers, the initial impulse to buy this book may not be easy to recall at this moment. Consider this for a little while, since you may gain important information to guide you in selecting a direction to follow at a later time. Take out your journal and write your recollections and current thoughts.

(Remember that you may select an area of potential change other than daily meditation. However, for the sake of having an example in the section below, we will stick with daily meditation. So when you see "daily meditation" in the text, simply substitute the practice you may begin in the future such as prayer, a strategy for life simplification, or an activity from your blueprint. If you are in the precontemplation stage, remember that you don't intend to make any changes now. All of this consideration is about what you might do in the future.)

KNOW WHAT YOU'RE REJECTING
BEFORE YOU SAY NO

For anyone who has eaten a meal with young children, the exclamation "I don't like it!" (before a new dish has even been tasted by a child) may be familiar to you. Even though we're grown up, we adults often do the same thing, rejecting a new idea outright before we even know what we're rejecting. Many resourceful parents enforce a dinnertime policy of having a child try the food before deciding not to eat it. This same idea may be worth applying while considering a new focus-enhancing behavior. All we ask here is that you give a few of the ideas in this book a try before deciding not to add them to your life.

You may be interested to learn more about a topic introduced in this book. We have cited some books in the references section, and we encourage you to refer to them. Before you decide whether or not you wish to develop a focus-enhancing behavior, it may help to take a closer look. For example, are you familiar with the organized religions of the world? What do you understand about spiritual practices like prayer and meditation? If you are a "show me the proof" type of person, you may want to explore some of the studies we described in previous chapters. Before you reject something, consider that it might be helpful to know exactly what you're rejecting.

Additional resources exist for you to learn about focus-enhancing behaviors that you may wish to consider. If you have access to the Internet, the World Wide Web is a good resource for learning more about these topics. There are also courses and books on mindfulness,

world religions, yoga, meditation, prayer, or just about any other practice you can imagine. There are spiritual directors who are specially
trained to assist people in enhancing their spirituality. Clergy may be a
useful resource for learning more about particular religions. Community college classes are available for expanding your knowledge of many
other practices discussed in this book. Actually, doing this type of
research is a significant step in the process of change.

UNDERSTAND MOTIVATIONS AND CONSEQUENCES

Could there be a benefit to not making any changes in your life
right now? Consider your reluctance to examine certain areas of your
life. From where does this reluctance come? Is the cost of giving up
your attention to outside forces worth the price? Do you want to make
the choices about where your life is focused or are you content to leave
that in the hands of others? Take out your journal and write about
your reactions to these questions. Maybe your life is fine the way it is
right now. Maybe you would like to make some changes, but it's just
not the time to do that.

GUIDED IMAGERY EXERCISE

We would like you to try this exercise, even if you don't want to
make changes now. Or perhaps you have already selected a focusing
behavior to add to your life. In either case, we ask that you spend the
next fifteen minutes sitting in quiet meditation. Sit comfortably. Close
your eyes. Become still and direct your attention to the following
scene: Imagine waking up in the future of the life you truly want for
yourself. Spend this time in meditation observing without judging what
your life looks like. In your meditation, what do you do? Where do you
go? With whom do you spend time? What is your work? What is your
play? How is your individuality expressed? How do you derive deep
meaning? Explore this image of your preferred life in great detail. Now,
come out of your meditation and return to the present time and circumstance. What differences do you notice when you compare your
present life to the life envisioned in your meditation. Think about how
your current life is different from the one in the meditation. Consider
what steps you would need to take to bring your life closer to the one
in the meditation. Was your image in the meditation similar to the

blueprint and simpler life that you developed in chapter 3? Was it consistent with your values and spiritual beliefs, which you examined in chapter 4? Write your observations in your journal. In reviewing what you've written, do you see opportunities to make even some small positive change? Do you need focusing practices now (or in the near future) to help you move in that direction? Write about your insights.

Contemplation

"I know that I probably should sharpen my focus with a practice like meditation, but . . ."

If you are in the *contemplation* stage, you are on a seesaw between wanting to make a change and not wanting to (Prochaska et al. 2002). You may see that meditation (or another focus-enhancing strategy) would probably be good, but you're not totally convinced that it's right for you. You may feel like you are not ready to let go of old ways. You may have some interest in meditation but not be able to imagine where you would find the time to actually begin this daily practice. There could be a part of you that thinks you are interested in making a change soon, maybe within the next six months, but not right now.

You have reached the contemplation stage of change when you have awareness about the expected benefits of meditation (or another focus-enhancing strategy), but you're not ready (or don't know how) to incorporate the new practice into your life. At this point, you are on a fence that divides your current life from your more-focused life in the future. This is progress from the precontemplation stage, where you didn't realized that there *was* a fence. The psychological term for this experience, where you feel two opposite ways about a change, is *ambivalence*. It is important to know that this is normal, and that it's necessary to embrace your ambivalence and be intentional about addressing it if you hope to progress.

At this point, some people fall victim to taking action too soon. Ambivalence is tricky. At times you may easily recognize all of the reasons to begin your new practices. You mistakenly believe that you are determined to change, only to find yourself quickly dropping your new practices as the old reasons to stay the same come back into view.

If you approach the study of your ambivalence with curiosity, like a scientist, and document the valleys and peaks as they come into view, you can start to see the big picture. We offer a suggestion for how you can do this. As you complete this exercise, focus on all of your reactions—not just your thoughts, but your feelings as well (Rustin 1998).

PUT SOME FEELING INTO IT

You will benefit more if you include your feelings in this exercise. Emotions contain important information and are a vital part of this process of change. Simply listing the cold facts does not capture the depth of feeling that may also be present. At the end of this exercise, you will not be making a decision by simply counting your entries in each section. The emotional weight of your entries can ultimately make the difference in your ability to move forward.

First write in your journal the line "My fears or concerns about *not* developing my focus by _____ ." Add a line at the end, and on that line write down the practice you've chosen to examine. In this case, we'll be using meditation, again as an example.

Next, write down your thoughts and feelings about not taking up meditation. Remember, your feelings are a crucial part of this process. For instance, if you just wrote down the surface facts, you might come up with something like "If I don't learn to slow down, I'll continue to be stressed and rushed." This entry takes into account that you have a problem, but so what? What impact does being "stressed and rushed" have on you? Remember, because of the nature of ambivalence, unless you write it down when you observe it, you may lose it later when it can make all the difference.

If you can get more of the gritty feeling into it, you might write something like "I will eventually feel the deep pain of loss because I was not able to be still enough to really focus on my spouse and kids. I will miss out on many precious moments, days, and years that we could have had together if I had not been so busy."

Can you see how getting in touch with a deeper level of feeling can give you much more impact? This can make the difference between staying on the fence and making a change.

GET PERSONAL AND SPECIFIC

As you consider ways to improve your focus, what benefits do you expect and how would the benefits improve your life? Now is a good time to think about that question. Include some of that information in this exercise.

First, write in your journal the line "The good things about developing my focus by _____ ." Add a line at the end, and on that line write down the practice you've chosen to examine. (Again, in this example, we'll be using "meditating daily"). Be sure to write down how the benefits will positively impact your life. If you simply write something like "If I meditate daily, I'll feel more relaxed" it can come off sounding like a public-service announcement that can apply to anyone. Try to make it personal and specific. For example, "If I meditate daily, I'll be calmer, and I may be able to sit down and really enjoy reading to my children in the evening instead of feeling the need to rush them on to the next thing until bed time." This one still contains the facts, but this version is personal and specific. The difference isn't a simple matter of syntax. If you are able to personally relate to the information, you're more likely to be motivated to change. Write down as many benefits as you can imagine.

ACKNOWLEDGE REASONS FOR NOT CHANGING

This may seem surprising, but it is likely that there are some good reasons not to make a change. Unless you acknowledge them, they will likely catch you off guard. Even with highly destructive behaviors like smoking cigarettes, there are some positive aspects that need to be acknowledged. (For instance, smokers often identify that smoke breaks serve as a much anticipated and enjoyable part of their workday. This is a real benefit, since nonsmokers may not take regular breaks.) When considering your new positive behavior (daily meditation, for example), be sure to recognize and list all of the good things about not doing the new practice. There is an advantage to many negative habits, otherwise they would not have become patterns in the first place. Eating fast food, surfing the Net, and channel surfing all have the potential to serve a purpose in our lives. Now please take out your journal and list the possible reasons you might have for not changing. When you have completed this list, review the previous two exercises on ambivalence. Compare the fleeting benefits of not changing those habits with the advantages of living a life of more purpose and clearer focus. Then you have the facts you'll need to make a good decision.

SEEK OUT A GOOD LISTENER

Now that you took the time and effort to understand your ambivalence, and you have some awareness of the nitty-gritty of your inner workings, what will you do with it? Completing the exercise can help you move off the fence and get ready to prepare for action. If you need further clarity and direction, it may be helpful to discuss this exercise with someone else.

At this point, you may say that you have resolved your misgivings about making a change (daily meditation or something else) and that you're ready to move to the next stage. If not, you may simply need to live with your mixed feelings for a while before you are ready to move on. If the latter describes you, you may consider talking with someone in your life who is a good listener. Talk with him or her about what you've written. A good listener is one who can sit with you and really try to understand you without interpreting, judging, or advising you. If your friends are the types to readily offer advice, you may want to ask them for exactly what you want. For instance, you may ask this friend to just listen to what you say, repeat it back to you, and acknowledge that they understand that this is where you are today.

For some friends, the natural tendency is to try to impart wisdom and "fix" the problem. Advice like this is often well intended, but it may not fit because it is heavily biased by the individual's personal opinions and beliefs. This dynamic may explain why so few of us actually take the advice we are given when it's offered. It would be like going to an optometrist who writes the same prescription for all of her patients—the one that works for her. She gives this prescription to all of her patients who need new glasses, and then she wonders why no one wears them. That would be absurd. Be clear about what you want from your friend. If he or she can't do it, go to someone else. If you're stuck, consider seeing a trained listener, like a psychotherapist.

DON'T WAIT FOR THE BURNING BUSH

Some people describe significant experiences that are responsible for changing the course of their lives for the better. For those who have had these experiences, change is simple. "Right here is the proof I've been waiting for," they might exclaim. They may refer to the child who is miraculously healed after the parents prayed; the engineering student who transferred to seminary school after a nearly fatal auto accident that shifted his priorities; the troubled youth who escaped a childhood of poverty and violence to grow up to become a social worker. Many people in recovery from addictions cite, with complete conviction, the miracle of their recovery. These stories fascinate and captivate us. Wouldn't it be easier to break free of apathy if you could experience an occurrence like this? In reality, many of us will never have a life-transforming experience like that. For us, it is crucial that we not wait for that level of certainty before making a change. We must work to accept some uncertainty and move forward.

TAKE YOUR TIME—BUT DON'T TAKE ALL YOUR TIME

Time is limited. If you are not yet ready to take the next step, then take an intentional break. Plan to check back on a specific date to see where you are in your process. Your life is too precious to spend on the fence.

Preparation

"I'm looking forward to a more relaxed and focused me."

You are in the *preparation* stage if you can honestly say that you're ready to start daily meditation (or another focus-enhancing strategy) within the next month. This is the stage where you will reconfirm your decision to move forward and gather the resources you foresee needing to begin your new practice (Prochaska et al. 2002). Your ambivalence is now resolved in favor of growth, and you are off the fence. This is the time when careful planning will greatly improve chances for success.

Think of this stage as being like relocating your family to a new state. You have already decided that you want to move, your motivation is high, and you believe that your life will be better in the new location. It would be an obvious mistake to get in your car, drive to the new state and believe that your new life will begin without attending to any of the details like selecting a house, getting a new job, packing your belongings, arranging for movers, contacting the utility companies, and completing forms to forward your mail. In this example, you can see how premature action would probably result in failure. The same holds true for attempting to begin a new focus-enhancing behavior before you have gotten ready. Planning is the crux of the preparation stage.

DECIDE WHAT YOU NEED

What do you need to know about your planned focus-enhancing behavior? Are there remaining questions? Have you decided to attend a church but don't yet know which one? Have you decided to meditate daily, but not yet decided which form of meditation is right for you? Perhaps you've decided to stop channel surfing in the evenings between 9:00 and 11:00, but you haven't yet found a suitable new behavior for that time. You know the general direction you wish to take, so this is the time to narrow your attention to the specifics. Determine what more you need to know about your new practice. Learn as much as you can now. If there is a book you have on your shelf on the topic, now would be a good time to begin to read it.

SET THE DATE

It is also important in this stage to set a date to begin your new practices. Be realistic about this. Choose a day that will allow you the time to do all of the work of planning and preparing but that doesn't give you so much time that you lose momentum. Ideally, the date should be within one month from today. If this seems too early, make sure you are not still in the contemplation stage. The following exercise will help:

Please write the following in your journal:

1. Complete this sentence:
    "I, (name) _____ , am making a commitment to myself to begin to do (new focus-enhancing behavior) _____ on (action date) _____ .

2. Great. Now write this date on your calendar, planner, or somewhere that you can see it daily until you take action.

SPREAD THE WORD

Tell others about your plans. This will let you know whom you can rely on for support when you begin your action and will increase the external pressure for you to follow through. Let supportive people know how they can best encourage you. Is there anyone who can serve as a coach or partner in your efforts? If you are interested in beginning a practice of daily prayer, you may benefit from identifying a prayer circle. If you wish to practice mindful meditation, enrolling in a class in your community may improve your odds for success. If your plan is to increase your understanding of a particular tradition, sign up for a course at a local college or visit a church or meeting place of that denomination. This may improve your chances of success. If you wish to develop a deeper understanding of a chosen faith, identifying a spiritual guide with experience in this area may be beneficial.

Regardless of the changes you wish to make, there are probably people in your community you can ask to support you. Take the following steps:

1. Identify and call at least one person who can support you in your efforts.

2. Discuss with this person what you are planning, and ask if they can support you in the way you need to be supported. Be specific.

THINK AHEAD

Plan carefully how you will be incorporating your new practice into your life. If you plan to begin a program of daily meditation practice, when will you do it? Think through your plans to do some anticipatory trouble-shooting. Are you thinking about meditating in the evening after the kids are in bed? What are the chances you will fall asleep before completing your meditation? If you are serious about your new practice, doesn't it deserve more energy than what is left over at the end of a long day? Perhaps waking up thirty minutes earlier in the morning will give you the time and energy you need to succeed. Be deliberate in these plans. Think of the time needed as an appointment with yourself that you can't afford to miss.

Take a trial run first. Schedule an appointment with yourself one day this week when you will have the necessary time, energy, and support to practice your new behavior, such as meditation. After you complete your appointment, find your journal and record your answers to the questions listed below.

1. What did you like about this experience?

2. What did you dislike about this experience?

3. What, if anything, would you like to change to improve your experience?

Use this information to construct your plan to incorporate your new focus-enhancing behavior into your life.

Action

"I'm taking the first steps to improve my focus through meditation."

If you are in the *action* stage, you are now ready to start or you've already started daily meditation (or another focus-enhancing strategy) within the last month. You will know that you are in the action stage of change when you are ready and motivated to begin your planned new practice (Prochaska et al. 2002). By this point, you should be feeling that the new practice is right for you and that you have the plans and resources to follow through. You should now have the information, tools, and support you need. You have made the commitment to your new behavior and are ready to go. Great!

There are several considerations to review in this stage. It's important to follow these suggested guidelines because they will improve your chances of succeeding with your plans. In this stage, just because you are practicing the new behavior, the change process is not complete. There is more to be done to ensure that the new behavior is solidly in place.

REINFORCE, DON'T PUNISH

The benefits of meditation (or other focus-enhancing practices) accumulate over time. Then these activities generally become reinforcing in and of themselves as you experience greater clarity of focus. Before that inherent reinforcement occurs, you may need other encouragement to keep you on your path.

When you engage in your desired new behavior, reward yourself. There is ample evidence that positive reinforcement works in promoting new behaviors. As we said, there will likely be intrinsic rewards that come naturally from your new behavior, but they may be subtle at first or may take a while to kick in. We encourage you to also identify additional healthy reinforcers. For example, let's assume that your new positive behavior is to meditate or to read some religious text every day. Some parts of this new discipline will be enjoyable and self-motivating. There will no doubt be other times when you feel like you need to push yourself to follow through. You might make a promise to yourself that, for each day you complete your planned practice, you will allow yourself time each evening for light reading (just for fun) or watching an enjoyable television program. You can feel pleased with yourself for keeping your commitment and following through with your focus-enhancing behavior *and* enjoy guilt-free time with some planned entertainment. Your self-esteem will be bolstered, and that naturally feels good, and you will also reward yourself with an activity of your choosing.

A creative form of reward may come from agreeing to put away a certain amount of money each day you follow through in your practice. You can then donate this money to a charity that reflects or promotes your values or ethical beliefs. Then you can see the tangible benefits of your effort help to improve not only your life but also the lives of others.

Avoid punishing yourself if you don't follow through with your new plans. A punitive attitude will only lead to guilt, and guilt does not motivate positive change, only avoidance. Seek the lesson from your slip-up and get back on track. Say, "I slipped up, but I know why, and now I will be better prepared next time."

Be careful about getting bogged down in believing that you should not need to "bribe" yourself to do something. A bribe is doing something illegal to get someone to do something unethical, illegal, and/or against their wishes. A healthy reward for doing something good is ethical, legal, and desirable. So enjoy all of the fruits of your new behavior.

In your journal, make a list of the rewards you can provide to yourself for following through with your new chosen practice each day.

SCHEDULE

Plan when and how you will engage in your new behavior. If for example you plan to pray or meditate daily, when and for how long do you plan to do this? Treat this time with the level of importance that it deserves. If the practice is optional, then sooner or later there will be other demands that will get in the way of your new behavior. Try to plan so that you will have not only the time but also the energy you require. You may need to be creative.

We recommend that you block out a specific time each day, and that you don't waiver in this commitment. As we suggested, think of this time as an appointment. If you have an appointment with your doctor, you wouldn't just skip it because you'd rather sleep or read a magazine. If you treat this as an appointment with yourself, you are much more likely to follow through.

If you find that you don't have time for your new behavior, you must carefully consider what you *are* doing with your time. If prioritizing your time is a problem at this point in the process, you might go back to the section on budgeting your time earlier in the chapter or perhaps return to the section in chapter 3 that talks about simplifying your life.

GET SUPPORT

Tell people close to you about your commitment to follow through with your focus-enhancing practice. Seek support. This is the time to identify someone (if you haven't done so already), who can serve as a coach or partner in your new behavior. This support will increase the social pressure to act and can make the process much more enjoyable.

You can give yourself support in a variety of ways, too. Consider writing notes and leaving them around your house reminding you to use your new practice. Notes can be brief, left on your desk, in the pocket of your coat, or on the dashboard of your car.

Maintenance

"I am really changing."

If you are in the *maintenance* stage, you have been meditating (or another focus-enhancing strategy) daily for more than one month. The goal here is to have meditation become a deeply held part of your life. It is important for you to stay vigilant to avoid relapsing into old, unwanted patterns.

The maintenance stage is all about working to integrate your new practices into your life on a deep level (Prochaska et al. 2002). These practices have been in place for at least a month now. In this stage it's important to work toward a deep connection to the emotion involved in your new focus-enhancing practice. The novelty of your new behaviors may be wearing off, so you will need to beware of apathy. (If needed, add a little novelty to your practice to keep you mindful and engaged.) In this stage, deeper growth that comes from sharpening your focus can really take place. Pay attention. Notice your increased awareness and the changes that occur as a result.

EACH DAY, A NEW BEGINNING

Renew your commitment to this new direction daily. Beginning each day with a prayer or centering meditation for continued focus can help you to reinforce your commitment to pay attention to what is truly important to you. It can set the tone for paying attention to your emotional and spiritual growth. This practice acknowledges that you can experience something even more positive as your quest continues to unfold.

REWARD AND REINFORCE

Reward yourself daily. Doesn't it feel good when you reach out lovingly to someone else who is in need? After all, both the receiver and the giver benefit from charitable acts. Anything that feels as good as giving can be a powerful reinforcer to maintain your new practice. You might consider trying to build in this type of reward for yourself for doing your new practice. For example, each day that you pray or meditate you might try to identify one item of clothing that you haven't worn recently to put aside for a local homeless shelter. At the end of the week, you will have a package to drop off for those in need, and it will be a direct result of your new practice. You can see how this type of reward brings deeper satisfaction than doing something solely for yourself ever can. Try something like this to see if it has this effect on you.

Reach out to your support system for continued encouragement, and consider mentoring someone who is where you were at one point.

In 12-step programs people emphasize reaching out to those at earlier stages. You may find continued renewal through serving as a coach or teacher to someone who is on a similar journey.

Termination

"This is who I am."

If you are in the *termination* stage of change, you could say that the change has been firmly in place for at least six months, and you don't see a danger of returning to old behaviors (Prochaska et al. 2002). If you are in this stage, going back to your old patterns may not seem likely.

At some point, after working in the maintenance stage for a while, many people progress to the point where the new behavior is as natural as breathing. Sometimes they cannot imagine going back to the way life was prior to their change. While lapses are possible, they aren't too common. This stage may be considered the end of the process of change but not the end of your growth. We suggest you stay alert to conditions and attitudes that may threaten your clarity of focus. We will discuss those soon.

It's a mistake to think that your new focus-enhancing behavior only applies to the workplace, to home life, or to any other isolated space in your life. This practice is more than a technique to use to deal with tough situations. The habit of managing your attention can be life changing and have a powerful impact. Periodically revise your practice to keep it novel. Remember, novelty helps us stay mindful. Invite yourself to make each of the precious moments of life steps toward greater meaning. Why waste your finite allotment of steps walking in place? That only limits your journey.

Recycling

"I'm learning important lessons about myself."

It will be unlikely for you to progress through these stages in a linear fashion. Many people experience setbacks along the way, and you may too. There may be times when you waver in your motivation.

This is normal and to be expected. If this happens, don't give up. Rocky periods are to be expected and are called the *recycling* stage (Prochaska et al. 2002).

In our experience, people don't gain wisdom during times of smooth sailing. Wisdom comes by navigating through difficulty. Like it or not, you can probably expect to slip up along the way. If handled properly, these lapses can be helpful. The challenge here is to learn from the setback so you can avoid repeating the same mistakes in the future. We often learn more from our failures than from our successes. If we don't learn from our mistakes, we're likely to repeat them again and again. Work on avoiding lapses; but when they happen, try to view them as learning opportunities.

GENERAL POINTERS

Now that you have a handle on the stages of change and what to expect, let's look at some pointers to help you stay on track in whatever stage you find yourself. Remember to keep your expectations realistic, seek support for your changes, and nurture your experience of gratitude and generosity.

Speak with people who have made focus-enhancing changes like you are considering. Learn from them how they stay motivated to continue. Some meditators tell us that regular meditation provides them with energy and clarity, as they make decisions about where to direct their time and focus. We have friends who frequently pray for guidance. This practice helps them remain calm and focused throughout each day. Clergy, spiritual directors, or meditation instructors can be good resources for insight and encouragement. Reading books about practitioners of a focus-enhancing path that interests you will likely add depth to this exploration. Visit a library or bookstore or go to an online chat room devoted to a practice of interest to you.

Avoid complacency about your practice of daily meditation or other changes you are making. Since your focus determines the quality of your life, please guard it with the attention it deserves. The following list includes conditions and attitudes that may alter your efforts to stay focused.

Vacations

Any change in routine that interferes with your schedule is a threat to maintaining your focus. This is one of the most common times when a positive-change program falls apart. Think of all of the diets, exercise programs, or other healthy living activities that fell apart over the holidays or on a vacation away from home. Plan for these times carefully.

Grandiosity or a "Holier Than Thou" Attitude

It will feel good when you are focusing your attention and taking the type of initiative that you weren't sure you had. It's important to avoid judging people who lack this type of intense focus. Notice if you are judging someone, then make a decision about how to react. Getting on your high horse and sitting in judgment of others will hold you back. Being grateful for the gift of your focus will move you forward in your own spiritual growth. The choice is yours.

Guilt and Self-Blame

It is important to avoid guilt and shame for not using these strategies earlier in your life. Maybe you have lost relationships or opportunities because you lacked a clear focus on what makes your life meaningful. Guilt feels lousy, saps energy needed to progress, and does not motivate change. Negative feelings like guilt alert us when there is something that may need fixing. Pay attention to feelings, as they have the potential to instruct us to do something important. If you feel guilt, ask yourself this question: Am I doing anything wrong right now? If so, how can I make it right? Do what you can to right your wrong, then let it go and move on. Harboring guilt is like trying to drive with a flat tire. Pull over, fix the tire, and get back on the road. Remember that the best way to make amends to yourself and others is to change your behavior, now and in the future. None of us can undo what we did in the past, but we have the capacity to live differently today. For example, if we hurt someone in the past, then we can make amends by helping that person. If the person we hurt isn't available, we can make amends by helping someone else.

Lack of Assertiveness

If you are faced with overt or covert pressure from friends or family to abandon your focusing practices, remember that you also have a right to your thoughts, feelings, and desires. If you try to live your life just to please others, you never get to live your own life. It's a tragedy to look back over your life with regret. This sense of waste is the retirement gift for the lifelong people pleaser. Please don't let it be yours. (Appendix B includes guidelines for increasing assertiveness.)

Expect that there may be lapses along the way. Don't get stuck in guilt or hopelessness. Try to learn from the experience and get back on track. Use your slip-ups as gifts since they are opportunities to learn something important about yourself—something you need to know to move forward.

THE REWARDS OF CHANGING

The process of making any type of change can be challenging, but if it is approached with preparation and realistic expectations, there is great potential for life-affirming rewards. As you think back over successful changes you have made throughout your life, you may be able to identify how you unknowingly worked through the process of change that we described in this chapter. Hopefully, you will be able to see that when you were unsuccessful in attempts, it was simply because you tried to change the behavior before you were adequately prepared. You now see the importance of doing the groundwork. This includes gaining awareness, resolving mixed feelings, and gathering the resources needed for change. By seeing the process of change in a systematic way, it is easier to identify where you are today and where you want to go and begin to take the steps to get there. We highly recommend the book *Changing for Good: A Revolutionary Six-Stage Program for Overcoming Bad Habits and Moving Your Life Positively Forward* (Prochaska et al. 2002).

As always, we recommend that you be patient with yourself, reward yourself along the way, and stop often to review your progress. As we suggested in the beginning of the chapter, it may be helpful to re-read this chapter. Now that you have the big picture, it may be easier to identify where you are and how you can increase your motivation to continue your progress. Change is guaranteed in life. The direction of that change is often up to you. Stay focused.

The End and
the Beginning

The light that puts out our eyes is darkness to us.
Only that day dawns to which we are awake.
There is more day to dawn.
The sun is but a morning star.

—Henry David Thoreau*

It seems appropriate to end our book on this note from Thoreau. We covered much territory and, hopefully, we stimulated you to read, meditate, and focus on how to use your precious daily allotment of attention to live a life of meaning, happiness, and well-being.

---

* Reprinted by permission of Random House, Inc.

We have some questions for you. How did you approach this book? Did you read it from cover to cover first and then return to do some of the exercises? Did you read just a chapter or two to assess whether the book was worth your time and effort? Will completing some of the exercises be an ongoing process for you, now and in the future? It may be helpful to pause and write about your thoughts and feelings in your journal before we go any further.

If you recall, we started the introduction to the book with a quote from Emerson that talked about how our thoughts determine our lives. As therapists, this idea makes perfect sense to us. We see it confirmed on a daily basis. When we approached New Harbinger Publications with a proposal for this book, we suggested the title "Your Focus Becomes Your Life." They preferred a title that defined the book more completely, so we brainstormed and came up with *Staying Focused in the Age of Distraction: How Mindfulness, Prayer, and Meditation Helps You Pay Attention to What Really Matters.* You must have noticed by now, however, that the phrase "your focus becomes your life" is a thread that we weave throughout the text. If you leave the first reading of this book with nothing more than a sustained awareness of this truth in your life, we will be satisfied.

At this point, I think we can agree that when we are cognizant of where our attention is fixed, and we are equipped with skills to redirect our focus, we will have more choices in life. We can opt for meaningful thoughts and activities. Undoubtedly, you will continue to learn more about how powerful your focus is in determining your well-being and the quality of your life. There is always more to learn about how to pay attention to what matters to you. "There is more day to dawn. The sun is but a morning star."

Appendix A

Self-Care for Well-Being

PHYSICAL

- Maintain adequate nutrition with three meals daily and snacks as needed.

- Sleep six to eight hours each night.

- Exercise fifteen to twenty minutes a day, three times a week.

- Follow a daily personal care routine.

- Abstain from tobacco and other drugs.

- Use only a minimum of sugar, caffeine, and alcohol.

- Balance work and leisure activities.

- Maintain regular physical and dental checkups.

EMOTIONAL

- Avoid blame, self-pity, and self-righteousness.

- Avoid extremes and all-or-nothing thinking. Start aiming for the mid-range.

- Recognize boundaries and maintain them.

- Remember that "No" is a complete sentence.

- Laugh and express joy. Play and have fun with friends.

- Practice mindfulness and stress-reduction techniques.

- Experience intimacy and tenderness in relationships with other people.

- Stop trying to control and fix others.

- Listen more. Give less advice and fewer explanations.

SPIRITUAL

- Acknowledge humility in not having the "right" answers.

- Laugh and express joy. Play and have fun.

- Enjoy art and music. Notice miracles in nature.

- Transform loneliness into quiet and peaceful solitude.

- Experience intimacy and tenderness in relationships with other people.

- Use the Serenity Prayer to experience a sense of well-being.

- Attend religious services or spend time alone focusing on spiritual beliefs.

- Contribute time and talent to the community, in particular those in need.

- Anonymously perform an act of kindness for someone.

Adapted from Hoffman and Hoffman (1998).
Reprinted by permission of Hazelden Foundation, Center City, MN.

Appendix B

Guidelines for Increasing Assertiveness

Become aware of how you express yourself, and then decide if you want to try to change:

Passive Communication Style

- If you use this communication style, you may take the outward appearance of the acquiescent peacemaker, but underneath the surface there may be anger at being taken advantage of and not feeling appreciated.

- People in the passive style are *dependent* upon the other person. They take cues for how to act and feel from their perception of others reactions.

- Review this list of traits to see if you use the passive communication style:

  1. I avoid conflict at all costs.

  2. I avoid expressing myself so no one gets upset.

  3. I simply agree with you (whether or not I really feel that way).

  4. I do something I don't want to do rather than risking conflict.

  5. I don't know how I feel about most things because I have so little practice with forming and expressing opinions.

  6. I avoid asking for what I need so no one feels imposed upon.

  7. I try to meet your needs instead of my own.

  8. I feel resentful that other people don't seem to care about me.

  9. I avoid expressing my ideas so no one is offended.

  10. I agree with your ideas no matter how I feel.

Aggressive Communication Style

- If you use this communication style, you may huff and puff and raise your voice a lot. On the other hand, you may appear as a sort of smiling steamroller, never yelling or appearing angry but intending to convince others that you are right and that they should agree with you.

- The aggressive communication style, like the passive communication style, is a style of *dependence*. This surprises some, but as long as your well-being depends upon a specific type of response from other people, you are dependent upon them and vulnerable to them. You may think you are strong, judging by the volume of your voice or the force of your personality. But because you must try to elicit specific types of reactions from others, they will always have more power than you, even after they say they agree with you.

- Review this list of traits to see if you use the aggressive communication style:

  1. I have a strong personality.

  2. I am a control freak.

  3. I try to persuade you to feel the way I do.

  4. I believe that you have to feel the way I do.

  5. I may speak with a smile and a gentle voice, but my goal is to convince you (the smiling-steamroller approach).

  6. I tell you what I need and coerce you into giving it to me.

  7. I need you to meet my needs. I have no other plan or option.

  8. If you don't meet my needs, you will pay the price.

  9. I will try to convince you to agree with my ideas.

  10. If you don't agree with me it's because you don't or won't try to understand.

Assertive Communication Style

- This is the ideal style of the three options presented here. If you use this style, you are respectful of others, and you don't require others to agree with you.

- The assertive communication style is the only one that is truly *independent*, meaning that the reactions of others need not deter you from what you want or need because your goal is within your own control. The objective is not to please others or to convince others of anything.

- The goal is simply to state the facts of your experience. When you want something, you can ask directly for it, and if it's not possible for the person to provide what you want, you are sufficiently resourceful to find it elsewhere. You can find another way of meeting the general need or can simply to do without.

■ Review this list of traits to see if you use the assertive communication style:

1. I know how to express my feelings, thoughts, and needs while being sensitive to others.

2. I appreciate different points of view.

3. I can have a disagreement with someone and still be okay, and I may even learn a new perspective.

4. I express my feelings, recognizing that others may feel differently.

5. I express my needs, recognizing that if they can't be met one way, they can be met another way.

6. I express my ideas, recognizing that others need not agree with me.

7. I understand that my feelings are mine. It is okay if you don't agree.

8. I understand that what I need is what I need. It is okay if you don't meet it. I can find other ways that are congruent with my values to meet my need.

9. This is my idea. It's okay if you don't agree with it.

10. I don't need to prove anything. I'm fine as I am.

Adapted from Hoffman and Hoffman (1998).
Reprinted by permission of Hazelden Foundation, Center City, MN.

References

Ano, G.G. and E.B. Vasconcelles. 2005. Religious coping and psychological adjustment to stress: A meta-anaylsis. *Journal of Clinical Psychology* 61:461-480.

Boomsma, D.I., E.J. deGues, G.C. VanBaol, and J.R. Koopman. 1999. A religious upbringing reduces the influence of genetic factors on disinhibition: Evidence for interaction between genotype and environment on personality. *Twin Research* 2:115-125.

Boven, I.V. 2005. Experientialism, materialism, and the pursuit of happiness. *Review of General Psychology* 9(2):132-142.

Brickman, P., D. Coates, and R. Janoff-Bulman. 1978. Lottery winners and accident victims: Is happiness relative? *Journal of Personality and Social Psychology* 36:917-927.

Bristow, W. 2004. *The Art of the Daydream*. London, England: MQ Publications Limited.

Bronson, P. 2002. *What Should I Do With My Life: The True Story of People Who Answered the Ultimate Question.* New York: Random House Trade Publishers.

Buber, M. 1975. *Tales of the Hasidim: The Early Masters.* New York: Schocken Books.

Buechner, F. 1993. *Wishful Thinking: A Seeker's ABC.* San Francisco: HarperSanFrancisco.

Burns, D.D. 1993. *Ten Days to Self-Esteem.* New York: HarperCollins Publishers, Inc.

Chamberlin, J. 2004. Open your mind. *Monitor on Psychology* 35(3):16.

Chodron, P. 1997. *When Things Fall Apart: Heart Advice for Difficult Times.* Boston: Shambhala Publications.

Corey, C.L.M. and J. Haidt, eds. 2003. *Flourishing: Positive Psychology and the Life Well-Lived.* Washington, DC: American Psychological Association.

Covey, S.R. 1989. *The Seven Habits of Highly Effective People: Powerful Lessons in Personal Change.* New York: Simon and Schuster, Inc.

Coward, H. 1986. Intolerance in the world's religions. In *Handbook of Religion and Health,* edited by H.G. Koenig, M. E. McCullough, and D.B. Larson. New York, Oxford University Press.

Csikszentmihalyi, M. 1990. *Flow: The Psychology of Optimal Experience.* New York: HarperCollins Publishers.

———, M. 1997. *Finding Flow: The Psychology of Engagement with Everyday Life.* New York: HarperCollins Publishers.

Davenport, T. H., and J.C. Beck. 2001. *The Attention Economy: Understanding the New Currency of Business.* Boston: Harvard Business School Press.

Davidson, J. 1999. *The Joy of Simple Living.* Emmaus, Penn: Rodale Press, Inc.

Davidson, R.J., J. Kabat-Zinn, J. Schumacher, M. Rosenkranz, D. Muller, S.F. Santorelli, F. Urbanowski, A. Harrington, K. Bonus, and J.F. Sheridan. 2003. Alterations in brain and immune function by mindfulness meditation. *Psychosomatic Medicine* 65:564-570.

Dossey, L. 1993. *Healing Words: The Power of Prayer and the Practice of Medicine*. New York: HarperCollins Publishers.

Dwyer, D.W. 1995. *Your Sacred Self: Make the Decision to be Free*. New York: HarperCollins Publishers, Inc.

Ellison, C.G., J.P. Bartkowski, and K.L.Anderson. 1999. Are there religious variations in domestic violence? In *Handbook of Religion and Health*, edited by H.G. Koenig, M. E. McCullough, and D.B. Larson. New York: Oxford University Press.

Emmons, R.A., and C.A. Crumpler. 2000. Gratitude as a human strength: Appraising the evidence. *Journal of Social and Clinical Psychology* 19:56-59.

Emmons, R.A., and M.E. McCullough. 2003. Counting blessings versus burdens: Experimental studies of gratitude and subjective well-being in daily life. *Journal of Personality and Social Psychology* 84:377-389.

Emmons, R.A., M.E. McCullough, and J. Tsang. 2003. The assessment of gratitude. In *Positive Psychological Assessment: A Handbook of Models and Measures*, edited by Lopez, S.J. and Snyder, C.R. Washington D.C.: American Psychological Association.

Everson, S.A., D.E. Goldberg, and G.A. Kaplan. 1996. Hopelessness and risks of mortality and incidence of myocardial infarction and cancer. In *Handbook of Religion and Health*, edited by H.G. Koenig, M. E. McCullough, and D.B. Larson. New York: Oxford University Press.

Fitzgerald, P. 1998. Gratitude and justice. *Ethics* 109:119-153.

Fowler, J.W. 1981. *Stages of Faith: The Psychology of Human Development and the Quest for Meaning*. San Francisco: Harper & Row.

Frankl, V.E. 1959. *Man's Search For Meaning*. Rev. ed. New York: Washington Square Press.

Gable, S.L. and J. Haidt. 2005. What (and why) is positive psychology? *Review of General Psychology*. 9(2):103-110.

Gafri, M. 2001. *Soul Prints: Your Path to Fulfillment*. New York: Simon & Schuster, Inc.

Gardner, H. 1997. *Extraordinary Minds*. New York: Basic Books.

Gerwood, J., M. LeBlanc, and N. Piazza. 1998. The purpose-in-life-test and religious denomination. *Journal of Clinical Psychology* 54:49.

Gilbert, R.S. 2000. *Building Your Own Theology.* 2nd ed. Boston: Unitarian Universalist Association.

Glasser, W. 1976. *Positive Addiction.* In *Integrating Spirituality into Treatment: Resources for Practitioners,* 1999, edited by W.R. Miller. Washington DC: American Psychological Association.

Grunebaum, M.F., S. Ellis, A.K. Burke, and J.J. Mann. 2004. Religious affiliations and suicide attempts. *American Journal of Psychiatry* 161:2303-2308.

Hagen, S. 1997. *Buddhism Plain and Simple: The Practice of Being Aware, Right Now, Every Day.* New York: Broadway Books.

Hamer, D. 2004. *The God Gene: How Faith Is Hardwired into Our Genes.* New York: Doubleday.

Hoffman, E.H., and C.D.Hoffman. 1998. *Recovery from Smoking: Quitting with the 12 Step Process.* 2nd ed. Center City, Minn.: Hazelden Publishing.

Hong S. and E. Giannakopoulos. 1995. Students' perception of life satisfaction. *College Student Journal* 29:438.

Huxley, A. 1944. *Perennial Philosopher.* As cited in *Integrating Spirituality into Treatment: Resources for Practitioners,* 1999, edited by W.R. Miller. Washington DC: American Psychological Association.

Johnson, R.A. and J.M. Ruhl. 2000. *Contentment: A Way to True Happiness.* New York: HarperCollins Publishers.

Kabat-Zinn, J. 1990. *Full Catastrophe Living: Using the Wisdom of Your Body and Mind to Face Stress, Pain and Illness.* New York: Dell Publishing.

———. 1994. *Wherever You Go, There You Are: Mindfulness Meditation in Everyday Life.* New York: Hyperion.

———. 2005. *Coming to Our Senses: Healing Ourselves and the World Through Mindfulness.* New York: Hyperion.

Kasser, T. and R.M. Ryan. 1996 Further examining the American dream: Differential correlates of intrinsic and extrinsic goals. *Personality and Social Psychology Bulletin* 22:280-287.

Kelly G.A. 1955. *The Psychology of Personal Constructs*. New York: Norton.

Keyes, C.L.M. and Haidt, J., eds. 2003. *Flourishing: Positive Psychology and the Life Well-Lived*. Washington, DC: American Psychological Association.

Koenig, H.G. 1994. *Aging and God: Spiritual Paths to Mental Health in Midlife*. In *Handbook of Religion and Health*, edited by H.G. Koenig, M. E. McCullough and D.B. Larson. New York, Oxford University Press.

Koenig, H.G., M.E. McCullough, and D.B. Larson. 2001. *Handbook of Religion and Health*. New York: Oxford University Press.

Koenig, H.G., D.O. Moberg, and J.N. Kvale. 1988. Religious activities and attitudes of older adults in a geriatric assessment clinic. In *Handbook of Religion and Health*, edited by H.G. Koenig, M. E. McCullough, and D.B. Larson. New York, Oxford University Press.

Krause N. 1995. Religiosity and self-esteem among older adults. *Journal of Gerontology* 50:236-246.

Langer, E.J. 1989. *Mindfulness*. Cambridge, Mass.: Perseus Publishing.

———. 1997. *The Power of Mindful Learning*. Cambridge, Mass.: Perseus Publishing.

Lepper, H. 1996. In pursuit of happiness and satisfaction in later life: A study of competing theories of subjective well-being. Ph.D. diss., University of California, Riverside, Calif.

Lesser, E. 1999. *The New American Spirituality: A Seekers Guide*. New York: Random House.

Levine, M. 2000. *The Positive Psychology of Buddhism and Yoga: Paths to a Mature Happiness*. Mahwah, N.Y.: Luarence Erlbaum Associates.

Linehan, M.M. 1993. *Skills Training Manual for Treating Borderline Personality Disorders*. New York: Guilford Publishing Inc.

Lopez, S.J., and C.R. Snyder, eds. 2003. *Positive Psychological Assessment: A Handbook of Models and Measures*. Washington D.C.: American Psychological Association.

Lyubomirsky, S. 1994. The hedonistic consequences of social comparison: Implications for enduring happiness and transient mood. Ph.D. diss., Stanford University, Palo Alto, Calif.

Lyubomirsky, S., K.M. Sheldon, and D. Schkade. 2005. Pursuing happiness: The architecture of sustainable change. *Review of General Psychology* 9(2):111-131.

Mahoney M.J. 2002. Constructivism and positive psychology in Snyder, C.R. and S. Lopez, eds. 2002. *Handbook of Positive Psychology*. New York: Oxford University Press.

Marlatt, G. A. and J. L. Kristeller 1999. Mindfulness and meditation. In *Integrating Spirituality into Treatment: Resources for Practitioners*, edited by W.R. Miller. Washington, DC: American Psychological Association.

McCrady, B.S. and W.R. Miller. 1993. The Importance of research on Alcoholics Anonymous. In B.S. McCrady and W.R. Miller, eds. *Research on Alcoholics Anonymous: Opportunities and Alternatives*, 3-12. New Brunswick, NJ: Rutgers Center of Alcohol Studies.

McCullough, M.E., R.A. Emmons, and J. Tsang. 2002. The grateful disposition: A conceptual and empirical topography. *Journal of Personality and Social Psychology* 82:112-117.

McCullough, M.E. and D.R. Larson. 1999. Prayer In *Integrating Spirituality into Treatment: Resources for Practitioners*, edited by W.R. Miller. Washington, DC: American Psychological Association.

McKay, M.D., M. Davis, and P. Fanning. 1997. *Thoughts and Feelings: Taking Control of Your Moods and Your Life*. Oakland, Calif.: New Harbinger Publications.

McLennan, S. 1999. *Finding Your Religion: When the Faith You Grew Up With Has Lost Its Meaning*. San Francisco, CA: Harper SanFrancisco.

Martin, P. 2000. *The Zen Path through Buddhism*. New York: HarperCollins Publishers.

Merton, T. 1979. *Love and Living*. Orlando, Fla.: Harcourt Bruce Jonanovich.

Midlarsky, E. 1991. Helping as Coping. In C.L. Keyes and J. Haidt *Flourishing: Positive Psychology and the Life Well-Lived.* 2003. Washington, DC: American Psychological Association.

Miller, W.R., ed. 2003. *Integrating Spirituality into Treatment: Resources for Practitioners.* Washington, DC: American Psychological Association.

Miller, W.R. and C.E. Thoreson. 1999. Spirituality and health in W.R. Miller, ed. *Integrating Spirituality Into Treatment; Resources for Practitioners.* Washington, DC: American Psychological Association.

Moore, T. 1992. *Care of the Soul: A Guide for Cultivating Depth and Sacredness in Everyday Life.* New York: HarperCollins.

Nakamura, J. 1995. The presence and absence of unifying themes in creative lives. Paper presented at the Wallace National Research Symposium on Talent Development, Iowa City, Iowa. As cited in C.L.M. Corey and J. Haidt (Eds.) *Flourishing: Positive Psychology and the Life Well-Lived.* 2003. Washington, DC: American Psychological Association.

Napier, N. 1997. *Sacred Practices for Conscious Living.* New York: W.W. Norton & Company.

Newberg, A. and E. D'Aquili. 2001. *Why God Won't Go Away: Brain Science and the Biology of Faith.* New York: The Ballantine Publishing Group.

Niven, D. 2000. *The 100 Simple Secrets of Happy People: What Scientists Have Learned and How You Can Use It.* New York: HarperCollins Publishers.

Norcross, J.C., A.C. Ratzin, and D. Payne 1989. Ringing in the New Year: The change processes and reported outcomes of resolutions. *Addictive Behaviors* 14:205-212.

Palmer, P.J. 2000. *Let Your Life Speak: Listening for the Voice of Vocation.* San Francisco: Jossey-Bass, Inc.

Pargament, K. 1997. *The Psychology of Religion and Coping: Theory, Research and Practice.* New York: Guilford Press.

Pearsall, P. 2004. The Beethoven Factor. *Psychotherapy Networker* Jan/Feb: 56-61.

———. 2003. *The Beethoven Factor: The New Positive Psychology of Hardiness, Happiness, Healing and Hope.* Charlottesville, Virg.: Hampton Roads Press.

Peterson C. and E.C. Chang. 2003. Optimism and flourishing. In *Flourishing: Positive Psychology and the Life Well-Lived,* edited by C.L.M. Corey and J. Haidt. Washington, DC: American Psychological Association.

Peterson, C. and M.E. Seligman. 2004. *Character, Strengths and Virtues: A Handbook and Classification.* Washington, DC: America Psychological Association.

Phillips, D.P., T.E. Ruth, and L.M. Wagner. 1993. Psychology and survival. *Lancet* 342:1142-1145.

Phillips, D.P. and D.G. Smith. 1990. Postponement of death until symbolically meaningful occasions. *JAMA* 263:1947-1951.

Piliavin, J.A. 2003. Doing well by doing good: Benefits for the benefactor. In *Flourishing: Positive Psychology and the Life Well-Lived,* edited by C.L.M. Corey and J. Haidt. Washington, DC: American Psychological Association.

Polivy, J. and C.P. Herman 2002. If at first you don't succeed: False hopes of self-changers. *American Psychologist* 57:677-689.

Poloma, M.M. and B.F. Pendelton. 1989. Exploring types of prayer and quality of life: A research note. *Review of Religious Research* 32:46-53.

Poloma, M.M. and B.F. Pendelton. 1991. The effects of prayer and prayer experiences on measures of general well-being. *Journal of Psychology and Theology* 19:71-83.

Prager, D. 1998. *Happiness Is a Serious Problem: A Human Nature Repair Manual.* New York: HarperCollins Publishers.

Prochaska, J.O., J.C. Norcross, and C.C. DiClemente. 2002/1994. *Changing for Good: A Revolutionary Six-Stage Program for Overcoming Bad Habits and Moving Your Life Positively Forward.* New York: HarperCollins Publishers.

Rahman, T. and A. Khaleque. 1996. The purpose in life and academic behavior problem students. *Social Indicators Research* 43:291.

Ray, O. 2004. How the mind hurts and heals the body. *American Psychologist* 59:29-40.

Roth, G. 1993. *The Wave: Ecstatic Dance for Body and Soul.* Red Bank, NJ: Raven Recording.

Rowe, J.W. and R.L. Kahn. 1998. *Successful Aging.* New York: Pantheon.

Rustin, T. 1998. Workshop 2B: Nicotine dependence treatment: A recovery-oriented approach. In *American Society of Addictive Medicine's 11th National Nicotine Dependence Conference proceedings.* Marina Del Rey, Calif.: American Society of Addictive Medicine.

Sacharin, K. 2001. *Attention: How to Interrupt, Yell, Whisper, and Touch Consumers.* New York: John Wiley & Sons, Inc.

Salzberg, S. 2002. *Faith: Trusting Your Own Deepest Experience.* New York: Riverhead Press.

Schaef, A.W. 1999. *Living in Process: Basic Truths for Living the Path of the Soul.* New York: The Ballantine Publishing Group.

Schwartz, B. 2004. *The Paradox of Choice: Why More Is Less.* New York: HarperCollins.

————. 2005. Too many choices. *AARP Bulletin* April:14-16.

Scott, V.B. and W.D. McIntosh. 1999. The development of a trait measure of ruminative thought. *Personality and Individual Differences* 26:1045.

Segal, J.M. 1999. *Graceful Simplicity: The Philosophy and Politics of the Alternative American Dream.* Berkeley, Calif.: University of California Press.

Seligman, M.E.P. 1975. *Helplessness: On Depression, Development and Death.* San Francisco: Freeman.

————. 1992. *Learned Optimism: How to Change Your Mind and Your Life.* New York: Pocket Books.

————. 2002. *Authentic Happiness: Using the New Positive Psychology to Realize Your Potential for Lasting Fulfillment.* New York: Free Press.

————. 2003. Foreword: The past and the future of positive psychology. In *Flourishing: Positive Psychology and the Life Well-Lived,* edited by C.L.M. Corey and J. Haidt. Washington DC: American Psychological Association.

Sethi, S. and M.E.P. Seligman. 1993. Optimism and fundamentalism. *Psychological Science* 4:256-259.

―――. 1994. The hope of fundamentalists. *Psychological Science* 5:58.

Sewald, P., ed. 2003. *Wisdom from the Monastery: A Program of Spiritual Healing.* Munchen, Germany: Random House.

Sinetar, M. 1987. *Do What You Love and the Money Will Follow: Discovering Your Right Livelihood.* New York: Random House, Inc.

Smith, H. 1991. *The World's Religions.* New York: HarperCollins Publishing.

Snyder, C.R. and S. Lopez, eds. 2002. *Handbook of Positive Psychology.* New York: Oxford University Press.

St. James, E. 1996. *Living the Simple Life: A Guide to Scaling Down and Enjoying More.* New York: Hyperion.

Stark R. 1996. Religion as context: Hellfire and delinquency one more time. *Sociology of Religion* 57:163-173.

Suh, E., E. Diener, and F. Fujita. 1996. Events and subjective well-being: Only recent events matter. *Journal of Personality and Social Psychology* 70:1091-1102.

Thich Nhat Hanh. 1987. *Being Peace.* Berkeley, Calif.: Parallax Press.

―――. 2003. *Creating True Peace: Ending Violence in Yourself, Your Family, Your Community and the World.* New York: Free Press.

―――. 1975. *The Miracle of Mindfulness.* Boston: Beacon Press Books.

Tolle, E. 1994. *The Power of Now: A Guide to Spiritual Enlightenment.* Novato, Calif.: New World Library.

Tonigan, J.S., R.T. Toscova, and G.J. Connors. 2003. Spirituality and the 12-step programs: A guide for clinicians. In *Integrating Spirituality into Treatment: Resources for Practitioners,* edited by W.R. Miller. Washington, DC: American Psychological Association.

U.S. Postal Service Annual Reports 2001–2004. Data on Direct Mail.

WHOQOL Group. 1995. The World Health Organization of Life Assessment (WHOQOL): Position paper from the World Health Organization. *Social Science and Medicine* 41:1403-1409.

————. 1998. The World Health Organization Quality of Life Assessment (WHOQOL): Development and general psychometric properties. *Social Science and Medicine* 46:1269-1585.

Whylie, M.S. and R. Simon. 2004. The power of paying attention: What Jon Kabat-Zinn has against spirituality. *Psychotherapy Networker.* November/December:59-67.

Wise, N. 2002. *A Big New Free Happy Unusual Life: Self-Expression and Spiritual Practice for Those Who Have Time for Neither.* New York: Broadway Books.

Woodruff, P. 2001. *Reverence: Renewing a Forgotten Virtue.* New York: Oxford University Press.

Worthington, E. 2001. *Five Steps to Forgiveness: The Art and Science of Forgiveness.* New York: Crown Publishers.

Wrzesniewski, A, P. Rozin, and G. Bennett. 2003. Working, playing and eating: Making the most of most moments In *Flourishing: Positive Psychology and the Life Well-Lived,* edited by C.L.M. Corey and J. Haidt. Washington, DC: American Psychological Association.

Elizabeth Hanson Hoffman, Ph.D., is a clinical psychologist in private practice, professional speaker, and consultant who has given seminars and workshops nationally. She has published over thirty professional articles and two books for the trade. She is also a member of the following organizations: American Psychological Association; the Central Pennsylvania Association for Health and Care Planning and Marketing; the Harrisburg Area Psychological Association; the National Association of Alcoholism and Drug Abuse Counselors; and the Pennsylvania Psychological Association.

Christopher D. Hoffman, MSW, LCSW, is a psychotherapist, nursing home social worker, author, and lecturer. He is a member of the National Association of Social Workers. He has written and lectured on mindfulness, resilience, and interpersonal effectiveness. He works with older adults in community and nursing home settings at the Veterans Affairs Medical Center in Lebanon, PA.

Some Other
New Harbinger Titles

The Cyclothymia Workbook, Item 383X, $18.95

The Matrix Repatterning Program for Pain Relief, Item 3910, $18.95

Transforming Stress, Item 397X, $10.95

Eating Mindfully, Item 3503, $13.95

Living with RSDS, Item 3554 $16.95

The Ten Hidden Barriers to Weight Loss, Item 3244 $11.95

The Sjogren's Syndrome Survival Guide, Item 3562 $15.95

Stop Feeling Tired, Item 3139 $14.95

Responsible Drinking, Item 2949 $18.95

The Mitral Valve Prolapse/Dysautonomia Survival Guide, Item 3031 $14.95

Stop Worrying About Your Health, Item 285X $14.95

The Vulvodynia Survival Guide, Item 2914 $15.95

The Multifidus Back Pain Solution, Item 2787 $12.95

Move Your Body, Tone Your Mood, Item 2752 $17.95

The Chronic Illness Workbook, Item 2647 $16.95

Coping with Crohn's Disease, Item 2655 $15.95

The Woman's Book of Sleep, Item 2493 $14.95

The Trigger Point Therapy Workbook, Item 2507 $19.95

Fibromyalgia and Chronic Myofascial Pain Syndrome, second edition, Item 2388 $19.95

Kill the Craving, Item 237X $18.95

Rosacea, Item 2248 $13.95

Thinking Pregnant, Item 2302 $13.95

Call **toll free, 1-800-748-6273,** or log on to our online bookstore at **www.newharbinger.com** to order. Have your Visa or Mastercard number ready. Or send a check for the titles you want to New Harbinger Publications, Inc., 5674 Shattuck Ave., Oakland, CA 94609. Include $4.50 for the first book and 75¢ for each additional book, to cover shipping and handling. (California residents please include appropriate sales tax.) Allow two to five weeks for delivery.

Prices subject to change without notice.